DIRECTORY OF TRADITIONAL BUILDING SKILLS

DIRECTORY

OF

TRADITIONAL

BUILDING SKILLS

THIRD EDITION

Published by the

ULSTER ARCHITECTURAL HERITAGE SOCIETY

in association with the

ENVIRONMENT AND HERITAGE SERVICE

BELFAST

1998

First published 1994
Second edition 1997
Third edition 1998

Ulster Architectural Heritage Society
66 Donegall Pass, Belfast BT7 1BU
01232 330213

Text copyright © U A H S 1994, 1997, 1998
Photographs copyright © U A H S 1994, 1997, 1998

Typeset in Times
Designed by December Publications
Printed by W & G Baird Ltd

ISBN 0 900457 50 3

A catalogue record for this book
is available from the British Library

Front Cover: Photograph Courtesy of The National Trust

If you are professionally involved in any aspect of the conservation
of historic buildings and wish to apply for inclusion in any further edition
of this Directory, please write, requesting an application form, to:

The Secretary
Ulster Architectural Heritage Society
66 Donegall Pass
Belfast BT7 1BU

CONTENTS

FOREWORD

Any publication must be accounted a success when, after only four years, it calls for a third edition, 7,000 copies of the two previous editions having been distributed free of charge to those requesting copies. Once again, this represents a notable example of collaboration between organisations within the voluntary sector – the Ulster Architectural Heritage Society – and within the public sector – the Historic Monuments and Buildings Branch of the Environment and Heritage Service. It aims to answer some, at least, of the very numerous requests for help in connection with conservation matters received from the public by both bodies.

It is evident that public awareness of the architectural heritage of Ireland, north and south, is growing steadily. We welcome the publication, earlier in 1998, by the Irish Georgian Society, of its 'Traditional Building and Conservation Skills: Register of Practitioners'; and we look forward to the publication in the near future by Environment and Heritage Service of a 'Directory of Sources of Financial Assistance for Historic Buildings'.

One consequence of this increased public awareness has been a very welcome renaissance in many of the traditional skills, and also in the production of the traditional materials, employed in building conservation work. It is interesting that, on the one hand, this Directory contains quite a number of new names; whilst on the other hand, some craftsmen, overwhelmed by the demand for their services, have actually withdrawn their names for fear of failing to cope with this demand.

The Society, once again, owes a considerable debt of gratitude to the Environment and Heritage Service for financial support, for the contribution of its skilled staff, and for permission to make use of its technical advice notes; to the various contributors and conservation bodies named in the text for information and illustrations; to the National Trust for permission to use their photographs; to the IPRCA (the Irish Professional Restorers' and Conservators' Association), the Irish Georgian Society, and Historic Scotland, each of which produces a broadly comparable directory; to Matthew Slocombe of the Society for the Protection of Ancient Buildings for his introductory contribution on maintenance; to Dawson Stelfox for preparing chapter introductions; and to members of the Society's committee and staff, especially to Harriet Devlin (who has acted as editor), Sophia Chambre, Rita Harkin and Joan Kinch.

I hope that this new edition will give support and encouragement to owners of traditional buildings who share the Society's anxiety that this invaluable legacy should be maintained and restored to the very highest standards.

C E B Brett
President, UAHS

INTRODUCTION

It is reassuring to realise that despite modern technology, an owner with common sense and respect for the traditional materials and construction methods of a building is its greatest asset. When a building needs more than simple repair, however, it is important to use a professional practitioner to give correct guidance. The Department of the Environment encourages this by offering a high level of grant aid on professional fees incurred during the course of a building contract on many buildings which are listed or within a Conservation Area.

Satisfactory repair requires a craftsman of proven ability. The Directory is based on information recently supplied to the Society by the organisations and individuals concerned and lists people who have experience of working with historic buildings. However, whilst great care has been taken in the compilation of the Directory of Traditional Building Skills, the Ulster Architectural Heritage Society cannot accept any responsibility for the accuracy of its contents, for the consequences of using this information; or for poor workmanship carried out by any of the practitioners or contractors listed here. The Society is unable to give specific recommendations nor does the inclusion of an individual or firm in the Directory imply any form of accreditation by the Society or by the Environment and Heritage Service. The details given under 'Membership' may, in some cases, include organisations which accept members without examination. However, while they cannot always be used as a guide to expertise, such memberships generally indicate a commitment to good standards of practice.

Listed under 'Examples of Work' are a selection of projects which, in most cases, have been completed in the last five years. This section is intended to provide the reader with some information on the type and range of work undertaken. The letters (L) or (M) indicate that the building cited is 'listed' or a 'scheduled monument'. Such structures are protected by law from inappropriate alterations in recognition of their special architectural or archaeological significance. The date given denotes the year in which the project was completed. Where the name of a practitioner is cited under an example of work, this does not indicate that a specific recommendation is being given. The UAHS ref. no. refers to the database of Traditional Building Skills & Craftsmen held on computer at The Ulster Architectural Heritage Society.

Readers are reminded that Listed Building Consent is required before starting any work on a listed building which may alter its character – this covers any changes to the interior as well as the exterior, and includes replacing windows and doors. Further information about listed buildings can be obtained from Environment and Heritage Service: Built Heritage, 5–33 Hill Street, Belfast BT1 2LA, tel. 01232 235000, fax. 01232 543111.

Buildings in Conservation Areas are also protected, and advice should always be sought from the local Divisional Planning Office before starting work.

Advice about grants and other assistance is given in Appendix 2 on page 204, and a list of useful addresses and telephone numbers is given in Appendix 3 on page 206.

DO'S AND DON'TS IN MAINTAINING AN OLD BUILDING

Old buildings are more than bricks, stone, mud and mortar. In them we have material evidence of the past and a visual asset for the present and future. Inappropriate alteration or repair can cause great damage to the character and interest of these structures. Current legislation should prevent demolition and more extreme forms of alteration to the exteriors and interiors of listed buildings; but often minor works to listed buildings and major changes to unlisted historic structures are left to the owner's discretion. In such cases an appreciation of the building and its construction and the use of appropriate repair techniques will be of particular importance. Professionals with the traditional skills needed to retain the character of old buildings should then be consulted.

Most people now accept that it is important to protect those great houses and national monuments which provide reference points – either good or bad – in history. About the need to conserve more 'ordinary' old buildings there is greater doubt. Often it is felt that these structures have nothing exceptional to contribute in architectural or historic terms and that their retention is unnecessary and prevents progress. But more humble historic buildings do have something to contribute, both on an individual basis and in a wider context. Frequently it is the simpler vernacular structures that form the architectural character of an area. Their materials, for instance, are likely to relate directly to the locality in which they were built in a way that modern structures made from mass produced materials often do not. Their form may well indicate their previous use and through this the past commercial or social role of the area in which they stand. Individually, although perhaps unremarkable, they are likely to contain evidence of design and craftsmanship generally not found in modern, mechanised construction. For instance the proportions of a classical facade, the undulations in old plaster and glass or the variations in colour and texture of hand-thrown bricks and tiles are all worthy of appreciation.

To look after an old building in a careful and sensitive manner requires some knowledge of its history and constructional form. It also involves regular maintenance and the ability to distinguish ageing, which is gradual and pleasing, from growing problems. This may sound complicated but, with some good basic information combined with common sense, an appropriate approach should be possible.

There are some significant differences between traditional and modern forms of construction which should be appreciated as the basis for understanding an old building. A full explanation of this subject is not possible here – information such as the Society for the Protection of Ancient Buildings pamphlet *The need for old buildings to 'breathe'* can help with this – but some of the fundamental differences include solid rather than cavity wall construction, the absence of modern forms of damp proof courses and membranes, and the use of 'breathing' rather than impervious materials. In essence old buildings normally have a 'softer' form of construction which allows a greater amount of structural movement and migration of moisture. This may sound alarming, but problems are only likely to arise if maintenance is inadequate, if incompatible modern materials are introduced (such as hard cement mortars, plasters and renders which hinder the evaporation of moisture unlike traditional lime-based mortars which allow it to take place) or if structural alterations are made which interfere with the way in which a building was intended to perform.

Roofs, Chimneys and Rainwater Disposal

Ensuring effective rainwater disposal is a crucial part of good maintenance. Water should be rapidly channelled away from roofs or other surfaces so that there is no risk of unwanted moisture penetrating the structure. It is also essential that there is a satisfactory means of taking water away from the base of the building so that it does not affect foundations or cause decay through excessive 'splash back' onto the walls.

Roof coverings are often attractive as well as functional elements of a building. Wherever possible traditional materials should be used for re-covering roofs. This should apply not only to slates and tiles, where natural/handmade types are greatly preferable, but also to thatch which should be appropriate to the locality in terms of material and detail. Slipped slates and tiles, copings to gable ends and the gradual decay of thatch should all be watched and remedial action taken when necessary.

The condition of gutters and downpipes should be regularly monitored; occasional inspections during heavy rain showers can be a revealing way of seeing how the rainwater goods cope with water from the roof. At other times stained masonry is likely to indicate that there is a defect of some kind such as a blockage or crack. At regular intervals – ideally in the Spring and Autumn – leaves and other obstructions should be cleared. Heavy snow can also cause blockages and flooding as it melts – if this is of particular concern snow boards or other modern alternatives can be used to guard against potential blockages. Also to be considered is the condition of lead flashings to chimneys and junctions and other leadwork, such as to valley or parapet gutters and to door canopies or bay windows. Leadwork will not last indefinitely and ultimately will need to be repaired or replaced. The involvement of a specialist is then advisable.

Masonry

The masonry of a building is not merely the structural material between the building's architectural features; the type of material used and its treatment are essential parts of the building's character. Traditionally there was, in general, an intention to create a unity in the surface of the wall rather than to emphasise the presence of bricks or stones in the construction. Thus modern 'ribbon' pointing, which creates mortar joints raised from the surface of the masonry, is almost always inappropriate for an old building. Rubble stonework was very often unified by a coating of render and/or limewash. Where used, traditional specialist techniques, such as tuck pointing – where the irregularities of the bricks are first disguised by a mortar that matches their colour, and then this mortar is scored with a narrow line which is itself pointed to produce the appearance of a neat and slim joint – should be respected as an essential part of the character of the brick wall.

Regular checks should be made on the condition of the masonry and mortar joints. The mortar, traditionally lime-based in most cases, should be softer than the surrounding masonry. As such it is intended to be a 'sacrificial' element of the building where erosion will occur. It is usually felt that re-pointing is required when the depth of recession exceeds the width of the joint. The growth of vegetation near to and within the masonry also needs to be controlled as damage may result.

Any significant structural problems with masonry are likely to require professional involvement but the owner should watch for evidence of on-going movement such as the widening of joints. However, cracks and distortions are not necessarily a problem; in some cases they will have occurred early in the building's history and will not be a continuing cause for concern.

Windows and Doors

The detail of traditional joinery is most important to the character of an old building. 'Off the peg' modern replacement doors and windows can bear a superficial resemblance to earlier examples but generally they lack the interest of the original in terms of form and detail. Particularly unsuitable are modern units in PVC-U, aluminium or tropical hardwood. Even if they make an attempt at a traditional design they are almost invariably a very poor substitute; typical unsatisfactory details include glazing bars stuck onto plate glass, fanlights incorporated into doors, over-reflective double glazing and imitation sash windows where sashes pivot rather than slide. Contrary to some manufacturers' claims, there is also evidence that PVC-U does not have a great life expectancy. Timber windows and doors, if properly maintained, can last almost indefinitely.

Similarly old glass, including crown or cylinder types, differs significantly from modern forms. Old glass should be valued for its colour and texture; these factors can make a surprisingly important contribution to the character of windows. Retention of old glass avoids the mechanical, lifeless look that can occur with modern replacement fenestration.

Regular maintenance of traditional windows and doors should include repainting, lubricating hinges and other sliding parts and checking putty to glazing for cracks. If required, draught proofing, or secondary glazing can be installed without harming the fabric of an old window or door.

Interiors

Interiors of traditional character should be appreciated. Modern replacement fittings such as doors, skirting boards, fitted cupboards and door furniture are likely to date quickly and lose their attraction whereas a well maintained traditional interior will retain its interest and is likely to become increasingly important to the value of the building. In most cases there should not be any major conflict between modern living and the retention of historic features.

Evidence of internal decay such as damp patches, deteriorating plaster and fungal attack to timber may indicate problems connected with the building's basic fabric and disposal of rainwater; but poor ventilation combined with the evaporation of water from baths and kettles may be responsible for some of these problems. In all such cases it is necessary to find the problem and resolve it before further difficulties arise.

A basic understanding of the form of construction, careful and regular maintenance and the use of appropriate traditional skills and materials are of fundamental importance to the care of historic buildings. With this the building is unlikely to cause problems, and the varied qualities that contribute to its historic character, whether grand or humble, can be fully appreciated.

REGULAR MAINTENANCE CHECKS
a basic list

Exterior

- Roofs – check for slipped, cracked or missing slates and ridge tiles, decayed flashings and dislodged chimney pots and copings.

- Rainwater disposal – check for holes in, and misalignment of gutters and downpipes; and evidence of blockages, including drains.

- Walls – watch for new bulging or cracking of masonry; deterioration of brick or stone surfaces; cracking or detachment of render; excessive erosion of mortar joints; and control the spread of plant growth into, or at the base of walls.

- Joinery and paintwork – check for flaking paint and cracking timber to doors, windows, bargeboards etc.

- Windows – look for damage to panes, and for cracked putty.

Interior

- Roofspace – look for evidence of water penetration.

- Walls and ceilings – check plaster for damp or deteriorating patches and for the efflorescence of salts. These may indicate damp problems, requiring investigation.

- Timbers and joinery – look for evidence of fungal growth on, or connected with timber. A mouldy smell may indicate decay, as in some circumstances may springy timber floors . As fungal attack is most likely in dark, poorly ventilated areas, check cupboards and under stair areas, etc. Also, look for evidence of new beetle attack such as frass: adult beetles usually emerge from timber between May and August.

- Pipework – check water and heating pipes (particularly in areas not normally seen) for evidence of leaking joints.

Matthew Slocombe
Society for the Protection of Ancient Buildings

ABBREVIATIONS USED IN DIRECTORY ENTRIES

(L)	Listed building
(M)	Scheduled monument
ACA	Association of Consulting Architects
ACE	Association of Consulting Engineers
ACIArb.	Associate of the Chartered Institute of Arbitrators
ARCUK	Architects Registration Council of the United Kingdom
ARICS	Associate of the Royal Institute of Chartered Surveyors
BIAT	British Institute of Architectural Technicians
CBI	Confederation of British Industry
CIBSE	Chartered Institute of Building Services Engineers
CIoB	Chartered Institute of Building
DoE (NI)	Department of the Environment (Northern Ireland)
EHS: HMB	Environment and Heritage Service: Historic Monuments & Buildings
FIEI	Fellow of the Institute of Engineers of Ireland
FIM	Fellow of the Institute of Management
FISE	Fellow of the Institute of Structural Engineers
HBC	Historic Buildings Council
ICE	Institute of Civil Engineers
ICHAW	Institute for Conservation of Historical and Artistic Works
ICOMOS	International Council on Monuments and Sites
IEE	Institution of Electrical Engineers
IEI	Institute of Engineers of Ireland
IFI	International Fund for Ireland
IHT	Institute of Highways and Transportation
IMechE	Institute of Mechanical Engineers
IOHBC	Institute of Historic Buildings Conservation
IPCRA	Irish Professional Conservators and Restorers Association
IPI	Irish Planning Institute
ISE	Institute of Structural Engineers
LI	Landscape Institute
M & E	Mechanical and Electrical
M.Cons.E	Mechanical Consulting Engineer
MAPM	Member of the Association of Project Managers
MAPS	Member of the Association of Planning Supervisors
MGC	Museums and Galleries Commission
MICE	Member of the Institute of Chartered Engineers
MIWEM	Member of the Institute of Water and Environmental Management
MRIAI	Member of the Royal Institution of the Architects of Ireland
NHBC	National House Building Council
NT	National Trust
PVC-U	unplasticised polyvinyl chloride

Reg. Architect	Registered Architect
RIAI	Royal Institute of the Architects of Ireland
RIBA	Royal Institute of British Architects
RICS	Royal Institute of Chartered Surveyors
RSUA	Royal Society of Ulster Architects
RTPI	Royal Town Planning Institute
SELB	Southern Education and Library Board
SPAB	Society for the Protection of Ancient Buildings
TCPA	Town and Country Planning Association
TRADA	Timber Research and Development Association
UAHS	Ulster Architectural Heritage Society
UCATT	Union of Construction, Allied Trades and Technicians
UKIC	United Kingdom Institute for Conservation

Consultant – ARCHITECT

David H Anderson Chartered Architect
92A Thomas Street
Portadown
Co. Armagh BT62 3AG

Telephone: 01762 330632 **Fax:** 01762 350428

Contact: David Anderson

Size of Firm: 1–10 people
Works throughout Northern Ireland

Specialisation: Projects under £250,000
Conversion or change of use of property
Maintenance / repairs to old and listed buildings

Background: 5 years on site experience of major scheme of refurbishment at St Luke's Hospital, Armagh, as Assistant Architect with G P & R H Bell Architects

Membership: ARCUK, RIBA, RSUA

Examples of Work: 1996–97
Rathfriland Street, Banbridge, Co. Down
Refurbishment, conversion and extension of existing Victorian terrace to day centre

1998
Ballyfrenis Presbyterian Church, Co. Down
Conversion of church to private dwelling

Consultant – ARCHITECT

Arch-Aid Design Group
5A Holmview Avenue
Omagh
Co. Tyrone BT79 0AQ

Telephone: 01662 250071 / 242702   **Fax:** 01662 241131

Contact: Des Ferguson

Size of Firm: 1 –10 people
Works throughout Northern Ireland

Specialisation: The conservation & restoration of all types of traditional &
historic buildings
General architectural practice

Membership: RSUA, RIBA

Examples of Work: 1996
(L) St Patrick's Parish Church, Plumbridge
Complete refurbishment of external fabric to church

1996
(L) First Omagh Presbyterian Church, Omagh
Internal plaster repairs, treatment of dry & wet rot, & remedial
works to external fabric

1997
(L) Private country house, Dungannon
Major scheme of internal & external repair & refurbishment,
together with design & construction of new extensions

1998
Private dwelling, Omagh.
Major scheme of external and internal refurbishment

UAHS ref no. 446

2

Consultant – ARCHITECT

Barnes McCrum Partnership
21 Somerton
Dargan Crescent
Belfast BT3 9JP

Telephone: 01232 781889   **Fax:** 01232 781874

Contact: C A Harvey or S R Whyatt

Size of Firm: 1–10 people
Works throughout Northern Ireland

Specialisation: General architectural practice with particular experience in
conservation work & listed buildings

Backgrund: Practice formed in 1979, with a broad range of experience of
commissions in private & public sectors

Membership: Partners
C A Harvey – BEd., BIAT
S R Whyatt – MBIAT

Examples of Work: 1993
(L) Lancasterian Street, Carrickfergus
New heritage centre & refurbishment of adjoining premises – in
the Carrickfergus Conservation Area

1995
(L) The Manse, Dromore, Co. Down
Repairs & maintenance

1996
Church hall, Dromore, Co. Down
Re-roofing

1997
Market Square, Lisburn
New shopfronts in the Lisburn Conservation Area

UAHS ref no. 2

3

Consultant – ARCHITECT

Rachel Bevan Architect
82 Church Road
Crossgar
Co. Down BT30

Telephone: 01396 616881   **Fax:** 01396 830988
                                         01396 616881

Contact: Rachel Bevan

Size of Firm: 1–10 people
Works throughout Northern Ireland

Specialisation: Repairs & conversion of historic, industrial & vernacular
buildings with a particular interest in traditional materials &
energy conscious design
The practice is developing an ecological approach to building and
the selection of materials, & sees this as complimentary to
historically accurate conservation

Background: Qualified architect, MA (Hons) Edin., inc. module in
Architectural Conservation
Architectural consultant to Southwell Trust, Downpatrick
Experience in renovation & conversion of listed, stone tenement
housing in Glasgow & conversion of brick stables in
Worcestershire

Membership: RSUA, Ecological Design Association

Examples of Work: Coach House, Main Street, Hillsborough
Conversion of derelict coach house to private dwelling

1996
The Narrows Guest House, Shore Road, Portaferry
Converted existing house & barn, & constructed new buildings to
create 13 bedroom guest house – in Portaferry Conservation Area

ongoing
(L) Southwell Almshouses, English Street, Downpatrick
Conversion of art room to residents' common room & creation of
new garden – in Downpatrick Conservation Area

ongoing
The Old Mill, Church Road, Crossgar
Phased conversion of old stone mill buildings to private house,
incorporating conservation & ecological ideas

UAHS ref no. 4

4

Consultant – ARCHITECT

The Boyd Partnership
1 River's Edge
13 Ravenhill Road
Belfast BT6 8DN

Telephone: 01232 461414

Fax: 01232 461616
Mobile: 0410 857455

Contact: Arthur Acheson or Sandy Roy

Size of Firm: 20 people
Works throughout Northern Ireland

Specialisation: Architectural consultancy services for the conservation &
restoration of historic buildings; adaptation of historic buildings
to appropriate new uses; & repairs to historic buildings using
traditional materials & detailing
The practice provides consultancy to The Northern Ireland
Environment & Heritage Service and to English Heritage
The practice has refurbished a former sawmill on the Lagan as the
Belfast head office and welcomes visitors to the River's Edge
complex

Background: Chartered architects

Membership: RIBA, RSUA, MAPM, MAPS

Examples of Work: 1994
(L) Friends Meeting House, Kendal, Cumbria
Adaptation to house Quaker tapestry collection & general
refurbishment

ongoing
(L) North west of England
Consultant to English Heritage, relating to grant-aided repair /
conservation works to historic buildings & Conservation Areas

ongoing
(L) Finnebrogue, Downpatrick
Restoration & adaptation for re-use of listed house, stableyard,
walled garden & farm buildings

ongoing
(L) 19th century public building, Bedford Street, Belfast
Maintenance & repairs

UAHS ref no. 5

Offices also at 30 Lowther Street, Kendal, Cumbria, LA9 4DH, tel. 01539 721275

Consultant – ARCHITECT

Alastair Coey Architects
96 Sydenham Avenue
Belfast
BT4

Telephone: 01232 659184   **Fax:** 01232 659184
(will change October 98)

Contact: Alastair Coey

Size of Firm: 1–10 people
Works throughout Northern Ireland

Specialisation: Restoration & re-use of historic buildings

Background: Alastair Coey has been involved with work on historic buildings
for 19 years. He completed a two year Master of Urban &
Building Conservation at University College, Dublin in 1997
The practice has successfully completed many projects on Grade
A & B+ listed buildings, including works completed on phased
basis

Membership: RIBA, RIAI, IOHBC, UAHS

Examples of Work: ongoing
(L) Parish church, Dundela, Belfast
External stonework restoration
Contract value £750,000

ongoing
(L) Barons Court, Co. Tyrone
Ongoing restoration of historic fabric

1997
(L) St Pauls Church of Ireland, Belfast
Restoration and remodelling of gothic revival church

ongoing
(L) Killyleagh Castle, Co. Down
Restoration of historic fabric

UAHS ref no. 8

Consultant – ARCHITECT

Consarc Conservation
50 Stranmillis Embankment
Belfast
BT9 5FL

Telephone: 01232 381711   **Fax:** 01232 381688

Contact: Dawson Stelfox or Bronagh Lynch

Size of Firm: 35–50 people
Works throughout Ireland

Specialisation: Conservation & restoration of historic buildings of all periods
Part of Consarc Design Group (see entry under Multi-Disciplinary Consultancy) – architects, quantity surveyors & project managers

Background: Fully qualified architects, members of RIBA & RIAI
Extensive experience of restoration & conservation throughout Northern Ireland
Practice formed in 1995 as part of Consarc Design group, with experience of Hewitt Haslem partnership & Dawson Stelfox, Architect

Membership: RIBA, RIAI, RICS, IOHBC

Examples of Work: 1998
(L) Parliament Buildings, Belfast for DOE Construction Services
Total refurbishment of building including burnt-out
Commons Chamber

1997
(L) Hanna's Close, Kilkeel, for River Valley Development Association
Restoration of listed 'clachan' as self catering accommodation

1996
(L) Knock Methodist Church, Belfast
Stone repairs & cleaning

1995
(L) Belfast City Hall
Cleaning & stone repair

UAHS ref no. 407

Also: Consultant – Multi-Disciplinary Consultancy – p. 65

Consultant – ARCHITECT

Alan Cook Architects
Cottage Studios
6 Main Street
Crawfordsburn BT19 1JE

Telephone: 01247 853737 **Fax:** 01247 853344

Contact: Alan M Cook MSc., RIBA

Size of Firm: 1–10 people
Works throughout Northern Ireland

Specialisation: Experience includes work on listed buildings and buildings of historic interest in sensitive locations in Northern Ireland and Great Britain including private residences
Special interest in industrial archaeology particularly the linen industry
See also Acanthus website htpp:/www.acanthus.co.uk

Background: 25 years in private practice, with own practice since 1989
A member of Acanthus Associated Practices UK Ltd., A.U.K. network of conservation and historic buildings specialists

Membership: RIBA, RSUA, Acanthus Associated Practices UK Ltd., UAHS

Examples of Work: 1992
(L) Private estate, Helston, Cornwall
Full measured survey of C18th James Wyatt designed manor house
Design approved by English Heritage for orangery, swimming pool pavilion, entrance & music room

1992
(L) Beresford Row, The Mall, Armagh
Restoration of two, C18th Georgian houses & major new extension to rear, to form home for recovering mentally ill

1993
(L) Bruce Street, Belfast
Restoration of facade and concersion of four storey former linen warehouse in Conservation Area to form retail premises

1998
(L) Castle Upton, Templepatrick, Co Antrim
Restoration and remedial works as phased masterplan to grade A listed house

UAHS ref no. 10

8

Consultant – ARCHITECT

F M Corr and Associates
Chartered Architects
I Bayview Terrace
Londonderry
Co. Londonderry BT48 7EE

Telephone: 01504 261331　　　　　**Fax:** 01504 371985

Contact: Michael J Hegarty (Sen.)

Size of Firm: 1–15 people
Works throughout Northern Ireland

Specialisation: General architectural practice

Background: Two partners involved in substantial number of projects including listed buildings over an extended number of years
Works have included all aspects of specialist trades inc. stonework, brickwork, renders, slating, lead & copper work, metalwork, joinery, moulded plasterwork, interiors generally, & specialist windows & glazing
Both partners are past members of Historic Buildings Council

Membership: RSUA, RIBA, Reg. Architect

Examples of Work: Phases 1 & 2 completed 1996
(L) St Columb's College, Bishop Street, Londonderry
Restoration of dressed sandstone façade to 19th century school

1993
(L) 33 Shipquay Street, Londonderry
Internal & external refurbishment of four storey, town building, inc. new windows, re-pointing of brickwork, re-roofing & internal works

1996/97
(L) Public building, Londonderry
Restoration of early 19th century building including re-roofing, refurbishment of stonework & internal reorganisation

Phase 1 completed 1996
(L) Glenmornan, Co. Tyrone
Restoration of 19th century church – repairs to Gothic timber framed windows, internal refurbishment, external repairs & small ancillary extension

UAHS ref no. 11

9

Consultant – ARCHITECT

Maurice Cushnie Architects
Lismore House
23 Church Street
Portadown
Co. Armagh BT62 3LN

Telephone: 01762 335510   **Fax:** 01762 350387

Contact: Maurice Cushnie

Size of Firm: 1–10 people
Works throughout Northern Ireland

Specialisation: Conservation, repair & restoration of Grade A listed buildings, including environmental & fire controls

Background: 30 years' experience

Membership: ARIBA

Examples of Work: 1991
(L) Town Hall, Portadown
Major repair / replacement of all building elements & theatre modernisation & modification

1992
(L) High Street, Lurgan
Conversion of dwellings to retail shop, with major repair of external elements

1993
(L) Castle Ward Mansion, Strangford
Re-roofing, stonework repairs & pediment structure replacement

1997/98
(L) Whitehall Tobacco Works, Belfast
Internal refurbishment and external repair, replacement of all elements

UAHS ref no. 13

Consultant – ARCHITECT

Caroline Dickson Architects
34 Clarendon Street
Londonderry BT48 7ET

Telephone: 01504 265010   **Fax:** 01504 269973

Contact: Caroline Dickson or Tony Robinson

Size of Firm: 1–10 people
Works throughout Ulster

Specialisation: General architectural practice specialising in restoration &
conversion of listed buildings, with a particular interest in new
uses for historic buildings
Considerable experience in church restorations

Background: In practice over 25 years with wide range of work, working
closely with officers from Environment Service – Historic
Monuments & Buildings
Served on Historic Buildings Council for 6 years

Membership: RIBA, RSUA, RIAI, ARCUK
Diocesan Architect for Derry & Raphoe, former trustee Ulster
Museum, former member Visual Arts Committee of the Arts
Council

Examples of Work: 1991
(L) Clotworthy House, Antrim
Renovation & conversion to public arts centre

1995
(L) Gracehill Golf Club, Stranocum
Conversion of farm buildings to golf club

1997
(L) Drumcourt House, Co Londonderry
Conversion of stone barn to holiday apartment

1998
Lifford, Co Donegal
Conversion / extension of existing building & extension to
provide offices for Donegal County Council

UAHS ref no. 17

Consultant – ARCHITECT

Ian Donaldson Architects
3 Victoria Street
Armagh
Co. Armagh BT61 9DS

Telephone: 01861 522271   **Fax:** 01861 527947

Contact: Ian Donaldson

Size of Firm: 10–50 people
Works throughout Northern Ireland

Specialisation: General architectural practice
Restoration of Georgian & Victorian buildings
New build

Background: Has worked with listed buildings in Armagh, Monaghan & Tyrone areas for 25 years; for Armagh District Council, church bodies, private clients & schools

Membership: ARIBA

Examples of Work: ongoing
(L) Palace Demesne, Armagh
Work to the former Primate's Palace, chapel, stable-yard, glass house etc.

1994
(L) St Patrick's Trian Visitors' Centre, Armagh
Restoration of church, house & outbuildings

1993
(L) The Mall, Armagh
Restoration of War Memorial & adjacent paths, railings & trees

(L) Church, Armagh
Restoration & conversion of church & lecture hall, & refurbishment of basement

UAHS ref no. 18

Consultant – ARCHITECT

D S C Partnership
46 Avenue Road
Lurgan
Craigavon BT66 7BD

Telephone: 01762 322047 **Fax:** 01762 321722

Contact: Thomas J S Donnell

Size of Firm: 1–10 people
Works throughout Northern Ireland

Specialisation: Restoration and conversion of various types of traditional and historic buildings for both private clients & public bodies
Diocesan Architects for the Diocese of Connor & the United Dioceses of Down & Dromore

Background: Partnership formed in 1989 – the combined experience of the three partners exceeds 100 years, and has been developed by study and having to apply their knowledge to the practical problems faced in the projects for which they were responsible

Membership: T J S Donnell – RIBA, RSUA
R Scott – BIAT
W A H Craig – RIBA, RSUA

Examples of Work: 1992
(L) Hospital, Tower Hill, Armagh
Refurbishment of three storey block to provide administrative offices & ancillary accommodation

1994
(L) Church, Donegall Pass, Belfast
Remedial work to walls, roof & windows following bomb blast damage

1993
(L) Private house, Main Street, Moira
Restoration, conversion & extension of dwelling to form guest house

1994
(L) Community building, Lurgan
Remedial work to premises following bomb blast damage

UAHS ref no. 205

Consultant – ARCHITECT

W & M Given Architects
1 Waterside
Coleraine
Co. Londonderry BT51 3DP

Telephone: 01265 51111 **Fax:** 01265 51115

Contact: Robin E M Smyth BSc (Arch) QUB, RIBA, MRIAI, MAPS

Size of Firm: 10–50 people
Works throughout Northern Ireland

Specialisation: Community practice with experience in all building types
Photogrammetric & autocad surveys
Robin Smyth is particularly interested in listed buildings & the restoration of stonework. His thesis 'Market Houses in Northern Ireland' is held in the Linen Hall Library, Belfast

Background: Practice established in 1888, current partnership has total of 75 years post qualification experience

Membership: Staff – 4 RIBA members, 3 graduate technicians & 2 autocad technicians

Examples of Work: 1989
(L) Cornmill, Bushmills
Survey of existing buildings, production of restoration design & supervision of contract

(L) The Bridewell, Broad Street, Magherafelt
Restoration of Bridewell to form museum & tourist centre

1996
(L) Town Hall, Coleraine
Refurbishment & restoration following bomb damage

1996
(L) Commercial building, Kings Gate Street, Coleraine
Restoration of ground & upper floors with new rear extensions & new period shop front

UAHS ref no. 24

Consultant – ARCHITECT

Greeves Kelly Partnership
'The Workshop'
9 Linen Green
Moygashel
Co. Tyrone

Telephone: 01868 723616   **Fax:** 01868 722535

Contact: Noel Kelly

Size of Firm: 1–10 people
Works throughout Ireland

Specialisation: General architectural practice
Conservation, restoration and conversion of historic buildings

Background: The practice has experience of conservation projects, including ecclesiastical, educational, commercial and residential buildings, listed buildings and buildings in conservation areas

Membership: RIBA, RSUA, MAPS, UAHS

Examples of Work: 1996
(L) St Andrew's Church, Killyman, Dungannon
Essential repairs & maintenance, including rebuilding of top of tower

ongoing
(L) Royal School, Dungannon
Repairs & maintenance, alterations & extensions to listed buildings including gate lodge

1996
(L) Speedwell Project, Parkanaur, Dungannon
Provision of accommodation in listed buildings for cross community charity

ongoing
Caledon, Co. Tyrone
Multi element improvements to NIHE dwellings in and adjoining Caledon Conservation Area

UAHS ref no. 563

Consultant – ARCHITECT

P & B Gregory Architects
4 Crescent Gardens
Belfast BT7 1NS
Telephone: 01232 326548 / 328971   **Fax:** 01232 236159

Contact: Peadar Murphy or Paul Mongan

Size of Firm: 10–15 people
Works throughout Northern Ireland

Specialisation: Architects, planning supervisor, project managers
General architectural practice with particular experience in listed
ecclesiastical buildings & community buildings. Involved with
the conservation and conversion of existing buildings

Background: Practice established in c.1906
Senior members of the practise are qualified as project managers
and have completed the conservation programme organised by
Queen's University, Belfast and the RSUA

Membership: RIBA, RIAI, MAPM, Dip. Proj. Man., RSUA, Cert in
Conservation (RSUA)

Examples of Work: ongoing
(L) St Paul's Church, Falls Road, Belfast
Restoration and refurbishment of church

1998
(L) St Patrick's Cathedral, Armagh
Quinquennial inspection report

(L) St Malachy's Church, Alfred Street, Belfast
Restoration and renovation of church

(L) St Mary's College, Falls Road, Belfast
Roof repairs, treatment of wet & dry rot, repair & replacement of
truss ends, leadwork and rainwater goods

UAHS ref no. 565

Consultant – ARCHITECT

Nicholas Groves-Raines Architects Limited
Liberton House
73 Liberton Drive
Edinburgh EH16 6NP

Telephone: 0131 4677777   **Fax:** 0131 4677774

Contact: Nicholas Groves-Raines

Size of Firm: 1–10 people
Works throughout Northern Ireland

Specialisation: Restoration, conservation and adaptation of listed buildings
Sensitive new-build projects

Background: Born in County Down, Nicholas Groves-Raines has over 25 years experience and has built up a considerable reputation for excellence in design and an on-going commitment to the restoration of our architectural heritage

Membership: FRIAS, MRIBA

Examples of Work: 1989
(L) Moyglass, Springfield, Co. Fermanagh
Conversion of former school house to private dwelling

1996
Breckenvale Farm, South Belfast
Phased conversion of farm buildings to accommodate new conservatory, stables & workshop

1996
Dublin Road, Enniskillen
Conversion of retail unit from corrugated iron cement store to quality hand-made kitchen outlet

1996
Tollcross Mansion, Glasgow
Full restoration and conversion of grade A listed mansion and gate-lodge to sheltered housing, for the National Trust for Scotland

UAHS ref no. 568

Consultant – ARCHITECT

Hall Black Douglas
152 Albertbridge Road
Belfast BT5 4GS

Telephone: 01232 450681   **Fax:** 01232 738117

Contact: Stephen Douglas

Size of Firm: 10 people
Works throughout Northern Ireland

Specialisation: Quality of new design & sensitive approach to historic building projects
Joint winners of DoE / RSUA sponsored 'House in the countryside' design competition
Winner of ten awards for new Linen Museum, Lisburn
Advice & consultancy offered

Background: Partnership commenced April 1986 with three architect partners – Mervyn Black, Stephen Douglas & Rodney Hall

Membership: Five architects – RIBA, three technicians – BIAT

Examples of Work: ongoing
(L) Private house, Templepatrick
Masterplan for conversion of double courtyard of derelict farm buildings into nine dwellings

1990
(L) Lisburn Museum, Lisburn
External refurbishment, re-roofing, re-rendering & repairs to decorative mouldings, leadwork & redecoration

ongoing
(L) Parish Church of St Philip & St James, Holywood, Co. Down
Renovation & extension of former school to form parish centre – project on site

ongoing
(L) First Derry Presbyterian School, Mall Wall, Londonderry
Conversion & extension to former school to create verbal arts centre – project on site

UAHS ref no. 19

Consultant – ARCHITECT

Alan Hamilton Partnership
Hawarden House
163 Upper Newtownards Road
Belfast BT4 3HZ
Telephone: 01232 471374   **Fax:** 01232 656262
     Email: ahp.belfast.@dnet.co.uk

Contact: Paul Millar

Size of Firm: 14 people
Works throughout Northern Ireland from offices in Belfast and Londonderry

Specialisation: The conservation and restoration of historic buildings, including churches

Background: Practice established for over 25 years
Responsible for the conversion, extension & restoration of listed buildings throughout Northern Ireland, inc. churches, private houses & banks
Paul Millar is particularly interested in Victorian & Edwardian architecture. His thesis on Blackwood & Jury is held in the QUB library, Belfast

Membership: The two partners are chartered architects
RIBA, RIAI, RSUA, UAHS
Paul Millar is a director of The Belfast Buildings Preservation Trust

Examples of Work: 1987
(L) Victorian alms houses, Larne Road, Carrickfergus
Renovation of 33 dwellings in three phases

1994
(L) 17th century private house, Ballycarry, Co. Antrim
Roof repairs & associated works

1987
(L) Church, Knock Road, Belfast
Re-roofing of tower & stonework repairs

1996
(L) Sinclair Seamen's Presbyterian Church,
Corporation Square, Belfast
Re-roofing of entire church & renewal of all internal plasterwork

UAHS ref no. 27

See also: Kriterion Conservation Architects an associate practice of the Alan Hamilton partnership, tel; 01232 671114
Offices also at 18 Great James Street, Londonderry, BT48 7DA, tel. 01504 370017, fax. 01504 374794 Email: ahp.derry@dnet.co.uk

Consultant – ARCHITECT

HMD Chartered Architects, Planning Supervisors &
Project Managers
13 Queen Street
Londonderry BT48 7HB

Telephone: 01504 267143   **Fax:** 01504 265995
     Email: hmd@maidencity.source.co.uk

Contact: Martin O'Kane, B.Sc., Dip. Arch., RIBA, RIAI, MAPS, MAPM,
Dip. Project Management

Size of Firm: 10–50 people
Works in counties: Derry, Tyrone, Armagh, Antrim, Down &
Fermanagh

Specialisation: Architects, planning supervisors & project managers offering a
wide range of consulting services
Urban refurbishment projects; listed building consent advice;
detailed inspection reports; preparing detailed proposals & tender
documentation; & contract administration & handover

Background: Refurbishments of listed ecclesiastical buildings; newbuild work
in Conservation Areas; external & internal repairs to listed, public
buildings; & environmental improvement schemes in
Conservation Areas

Membership: RIBA, RIAI, APS, APM

Examples of Work: 1989
(L) Bank of Ireland, Strand Road, Londonderry
Refurbishment of listed building
Contract value £850,000

1995
(L) Bank of Ireland, The Diamond, Coleraine
Refurbishment of listed building
Contract value £400,000

1989 to 1996
(L) Various projects for Inner City Trust, Londonderry
New buildings in Historic City Conservation Area
Total contract value £9,000,000

1996
(L) Church of the Sacred Heart, Omagh
Refurbishment of listed building
Contract value £1,500,000

UAHS ref no. 26

Consultant – ARCHITECT

Isherwood & Ellis
15 Malone Road
Belfast BT9 6RT

Telephone: 01232 663291   **Fax:** 01232 682727

Contact: Kenneth Fleming

Size of Firm: 10–30 people
Works throughout Northern Ireland

Specialisation: General architectural practice – with associated building
surveying practice
Design and construction of new build, refurbishment, restoration
& conservation projects
Town planners, project managers, planning supervisors

Background: Practice established over 30 years and has been associated with
many restoration & conservation projects
The two partners are chartered architects and a director in the
group is a chartered building surveyor. Arthur Sloan has
completed the Queen's Conservation course

Membership: RSUA, RIBA, UAHS, Association of Project Managers,
Association of Planning Supervisors

Examples of Work: 1988 – ongoing
(L) Church, Antrim
Series of restoration, refurbishment & conservation projects over
ten years

1990 – ongoing
(L) Victorian commercial building, Donegall Square South,
Belfast
Series of contracts for restoration, refurbishment & conservation

1997 – ongoing
(L) Upper Crescent, Belfast
Restoration & refurbishment of property for office
accommodation

1994
(L) Courthouse, Crumlin Road, Belfast
Survey, report & proposals for refurbishment & restoration

UAHS ref no. 33

21

Consultant – ARCHITECT

Kennedy Fitzgerald and Associates
3 Eglantine Place
Belfast BT9 6EY

Telephone: 01232 661632   **Fax:** 01232 664532

Contact: J P Acheson

Size of Firm: 10–50 people
Works throughout Northern Ireland

Specialisation: General architectural practice

Background: Winner of RIAI Gold Medal

Membership: RSUA, RIBA, RIAI

Examples of Work: 1993
Ballyearl Arts Centre, Newtownabbey
Restoration of farmhouse for Newtownabbey Borough Council as part of new theatre complex

1994
8–10 Irish Street, Downpatrick
Construction of new commercial building in centre of Downpatrick Conservation Area, replicating design and materials of previous building on site

1996
(L) Shane's Castle ruins, Co. Antrim
Restoration of ruins for public amenity

1998
(L) Old Town Hall Development, Omagh
Restoration of High Street Building

UAHS ref no. 34

Consultant – ARCHITECT

Mary Kerrigan Architects
3 De Burgh Terrace
Derry BT48 7LQ

Telephone: 01504 261510   **Fax:** 01504 261510

Contact: Mary Kerrigan

Size of Firm: 1–10 people
Works throughout Northern Ireland

Specialisation: The repair of historic buildings promoting a 'conservation'
approach
Sensitive conversion of old buildings to new uses incorporating
sympathetic additions to a high standard of contemporary design
Traditional building technology & materials, in particular,
specification of 'breathable' lime putty mortars, renders, plasters
& pigmented limewashes
Experience of client groups includes community & voluntary
organisations
Building types include community / resource, educational,
ecclesiastical, cultural, residential, exhibition / visitor, public
houses, historic industrial

Background: Mary Kerrigan, B Arch., SPAB Scholar 1992, with 10 years
experience, including nine months travel throughout UK &
Ireland on SPAB scholarship, visiting & working on a wide range
of historic buildings undergoing repair
Hands-on experience of lime technology
Training includes a well developed understanding of SPAB
philosophy i.e. aiming to slow rates of decay & maximise
retention of historic building fabric by minimal intervention

Membership: SPAB, RIBA, North West Architectural Association

Examples of Work: ongoing
Church, Cahans, Ballybay
Conversion of church (c.1840) to geneology centre

ongoing
Garden House, Castlecoole, Enniskillen
Extension

1996 – 1998
(L) Nos. 3, 6 & 11 De Burgh Terrace, Derry
Schemes of internal / external repair, & new extension to no. 6

UAHS ref no. 453

ongoing
Claragh Farm, Ramelton, Co. Donegal
Conversion of farm building to house (18th C)

Consultant – ARCHITECT

Leighton Johnston Associates
15 Stranmillis Road
Belfast
BT9 5AF

Telephone: 01232 381738   **Fax:** 01232 381249

Contact: Stephen Leighton

Size of Firm: 5 people
Works throughout Ireland

Specialisation: All forms of building restoration & conversion
Building defects
Ecclesiastical re-ordering
Planning supervisors (CDM regulations)
Heritage Lottery Fund applications

Background: Diocesan Architects to the Church of Ireland, Diocese of Armagh since 1982
Member of Historic Buildings Council 1988–1994
Architectural advisor to the DoE for Moira Conservation Area

Membership: RIBA, RSUA, ACIArb.

Examples of Work: 1993–97
(L) Civic building, College Hill, Armagh
Major restoration & reconstruction

1996
(L) 11 Vicar's Hill, Armagh
Complete restoration of burnt-out Georgian terrace house

1996–98
(L) St Michael's Church, Castlecaulfield
Extensive structural repairs to tower and stonework

1998
(L) Saint George's Parish Church, Belfast
Stonework repairs and internal refurbishment

UAHS ref no. 38

24

Consultant – ARCHITECT

Julian Leith RIBA
32 Quarry Road
Lisbane
Comber
Co. Down BT23 6ED

Telephone: 01238 542032   **Fax:** 01238 542032

Contact: Julian Leith

Size of Firm: 1–10 people
Works throughout Northern Ireland

Specialisation: Rural buildings, renovation of old dwellings & other buildings
inc. public houses, hotels, banks & mills
New build & extensions within historic contexts

Background: Liverpool Polytechnic 1972–78, qualified 1979, worked in
Liverpool inc. Dock Development Scheme, joined Raymond
Leith Partnership 1983 & formed own practice 1990

Membership: RIBA, RSUA

Examples of Work: 1989
(L) Waterfoot, Glenariff
Complete renovation of former mansion house to form training
school adventure centre

1990
32 Quarry Road, Lisbane, Comber
Renovation of old stone cottage & conversion of adjacent barn to
form own house

1991
(L) Private club, Royal Avenue, Belfast
Renovation of bar area including new bars to match listed interior

ongoing
(L) Ballydugan Mill, Ballydugan, Downpatrick
Conversion of 18th century, eight storey mill building to
interpretative centre with bedroom accommodation and restaurant

UAHS ref no. 39

Consultant – ARCHITECT

Lyons Architects
117 University Street
Belfast BT7 1HP

Telephone: 01232 232001   **Fax:** 01232 247332

Contact: P O'Hagan or P Moran

Size of Firm: 1–10 people
Works throughout Northern Ireland

Specialisation: Project feasibility studies
Design consultancy
Contract administration & project co-ordination & management
Design & construction consultancy for historic buildings

Background: Experience of restoration & refurbishment of listed buildings &
the design & construction of buildings within Conservation Areas
National Housing Design Award, Tyrone Brick Award (housing &
commercial), London Docklands Commission Award

Membership: RIBA

Examples of Work: 1994
(L) Visitors' centre, Slieve Gullion Forest Park
Refurbishment & change of use of existing stable block to
exhibition area, restaurant & holiday apartments

ongoing
(L) Private country house, Portaferry, Co. Down
Phased improvement & refurbishment work inc. replacement of
external leadwork & reinstatement of internal plasterwork

1994
(L) Commercial building, Hill Street, Newry
Refurbishment of listed façade
Awarded 'Building of the Year' 1995

1997
(L) MacNeice Hall, Malone Road, Belfast
Comprehensive refurbishment of listed buildings, formerly
known as Aquinas Hall

UAHS ref no. 296

Consultant – ARCHITECT

C J McCauley RIBA
Architect
71 Osborne Park
Malone Road
Belfast BT9 6JP

Telephone: 01232 667468 **Fax:** 01232 382593

Contact: Christopher McCauley

Size of Firm: 1–10 people
Works throughout Northern Ireland

Specialisation: Conversion & restoration of historic buildings

Background: Responsible for the conversion & renovation of listed buildings including private houses, large public & community buildings, schools & public houses

Membership: RIBA, RSUA, ACA, ARB

Examples of Work: 1998
(L) Private house, Malone Park, Belfast
Conversions and extension

1998
(L) Tedford Chandlery, Donegal Quay, Belfast
Conversion, alterations to a restaurant

1995
(L) former Christian Brothers' School, Donegall Street, Belfast
Proposed guest house accommodation

1995
(L) Private house, Drumbo
Conversion of a former hall & caretaker's residence to a dwelling

1993
(L) Private house, Ballylesson Road, Drumbo
Restoration of house, including removal of unsuitable extensions[1] & alterations

UAHS ref no. 182

Consultant – ARCHITECT

McCormick Tracey Mullarkey
29 Clarendon Street
Londonderry
BT48 7ER

Telephone: 01504 265014   **Fax:** 01504 360047

Contact: Messrs J J Tracey or T C Mullarkey

Size of Firm: 1–15 people
Works throughout Northern Ireland

Specialisation: Conservation & conversion of existing buildings, particularly of the 19th century
Surveys, integration of new services into historic environments, coordination of structural & services consultants
Extensions to listed & historical buildings with emphasis on context, site & choice of materials

Background: Over 25 years' experience with officers from Environment Service – Historic Monuments & Buildings, experience of traditional building materials & trades inc. stone masonry, lead, thatch, ironwork, joinery, stained glass & artists

Membership: RIBA, RSUA, RIAI, UAHS

Examples of Work: 1993
Outdoor museum, Gortin, Co. Tyrone
Design of full size exhibits of Irish settlement types, built using traditional materials & skills

1990
(L) Church, Irvinestown, Co. Fermanagh
Extension to existing 19th century Gothic church, re-roofing, new walling & roof structure

1989
(L) Cathedral, Derry
Three phases of work inc. stone cleaning & repairs, re-roofing, new extension to Sacristy, interior improvements, repairs & lighting

1994
(L) Necarne, Irvinestown, Co. Fermanagh
Extension & conversion of existing outbuildings & yards at Necarne Castle to form major equestrian centre

UAHS ref no. 289

Consultant – ARCHITECT

McCready & Company Architects
8 Market Place
Lisburn
Co. Antrim BT28 1AN

Telephone: 01846 662357

Fax: 01846 662263
E-mail: mcc.co.arch@dnet.co.uk

Contact: Andrew McCready

Size of Firm: 1–10 people
Works throughout Northern Ireland

Specialisation: Practice of chartered architects established in Lisburn since 1949 with experience of acting as lead consultant, involved in the renovation, restoration & re-use of listed and unlisted buildings Sympathetic & cost-effective service with emphasis on contemporary conversion

Background: Diploma course in Advanced Architectural Studies (QUB) inc. 'Re-use of old buildings' conservation project – based on Brookfield, Moira (former Quaker Agricultural School)

Membership: RIBA, RSUA, ARCUK

Examples of Work: 1996
(L) 15, 17 & 19 Seymour Street, Lisburn
Conversion & renovation of former hospital (Antrim Infirmary) to self-contained flats inc. repairs to internal & external fabric, & major re-planning of interior

1996
(L) Eden Cottage, Pine Hill, Lisburn
Comprehensive renovation & restoration of thatched cottage inc. new extension to provide living accommodation

1993
(L) Baptist church, Millisle Road, Donaghadee
Renovation & conversion of vacant, former school to church inc. stone repairs and insertion of new gallery in main hall

1996
Drumgooland Mill, Seaforde, Co. Down
Major conversion of derelict mill to form dwelling designed around large open-plan living area, inc. stonework repairs & use of salvaged materials

UAHS ref no. 162

29

Consultant – ARCHITECT

McCutcheon & Wilkinson
18 Linenhall Street
Ballymena
Co. Antrim BT43 5AL

Telephone: 01266 49525   **Fax:** 01266 45791

Contact: Winston Boyce

Size of Firm: 10–50 people
Works throughout Northern Ireland

Specialisation: Architecture within a multi-disciplinary team including structural & civil engineers, environmental consultants, CDM planning supervisors & interior designers

Background: Architects for several award winning schemes

Membership: RIBA, RSUA, RIAI, MICE, MIWEM, MAPS

Examples of Work: 1992
(L) Heritage centre, Arthur Cottage, Cullybackey
Re-thatching, stabilisation of front wall & replacement of windows, landscaping & conversion of out-buildings to form heritage centre

1992
(L) Private mansion house, Ballymena
Restoration of derelict Victorian farm courtyard
Winner of RICS Conservation Commendation
Winner of Civic Trust Commendation

1996
Former cottage hospital, Ballymena
Conversion to 'Homefirst' headquarters
Winner of RICS Conservation Commendation

1998
(L) The Glebe, Ballynascreen, Draperstown
Built 1794, as a rectory, ceased to be lived in about 1972
Complete restoration of derelict buildings
RICS award (short listed – decision awaited)

UAHS ref no. 47

Also: Consultant – Structural & Civil Engineer, Environmental Consultant, Interior Designer, Multi-Disciplinary Consultancy

Consultant – ARCHITECT

Mackel & Doherty Architects
6 Kinnaird Street
Belfast BT14 6BE

Telephone: 01232 746386 **Fax:** 01232 351481
e-mail: macdoc@iol.ie

Contact: Ciaran Mackel

Size of Firm: 1–10 people
Works throughout Northern Ireland

Specialisation: General architectural practice with particular experience of listed ecclesiastical & community buildings
Site sensitive and user participation design approach to modern conversions of historic building projects

Background: S Mackel, senior partner, surveyed all the Court Houses in Northern Ireland & has subsequently been involved in a number of refurbishment schemes
C Mackel completed Urban Conservation Course over 1 year as part of an MSc in Urban Design

Membership: RIBA, RIAI, Architectural Association London, Architectural Association of Ireland, Association of Planning Supervisors, British Institute of Architectural Technologists

Examples of Work: 1990
(L) Antrim Road, Belfast
General repairs, external repairs & cleaning of stonework

1990
(L) Castle Place, Belfast
Shop-fitting, external repairs & stone cleaning

1991
(L) 222 Limestone Road, Belfast
Extensive refurbishment & rear extension to Pastoral Centre

1998
(L) Beechmount House, Falls Road, Belfast
Conversion of old peoples hostel into a secondary school building

Consultant – ARCHITECT

MacRae Hanlon Spence Partnership Chartered Architects
6 Malone Road
Belfast BT9 5BN

Telephone: 01232 664931   **Fax:** 01232 661659

Contact: Derrick MacRae

Size of Firm: 1–10 people
Works throughout Northern Ireland

Specialisation: General architectural practice

Membership: All partners are members of the RIBA

Examples of Work: 1994
11–19 Mount Charles, Belfast
Conversion of property in Queen's Conservation Area to student accommodation
Works included cleaning & pointing of brickwork, new roof & new sliding sash windows

1995
26–50 Mount Charles, Belfast
Conversion of property in Queen's Conservation Area to student accommodation
Works included cleaning & pointing of brickwork, new roof & new sliding sash windows

1995
(L) 161–163 Victoria Street, Belfast
Repairs & modernisation following bomb damage inc. sandstone repairs and reconstruction, new roof & new windows

1998
Crawfordsburn Hospital, Crawfordsburn
Conversion of hospital to apartments

UAHS ref no. 40

Consultant – ARCHITECT

MacRandal Partnership Chartered Architects &
Planning Supervisors
17 Malone Road
Belfast BT9 6RT

Telephone: 01232 669472   **Fax:** 01232 666008

Contact: Daniel J MacRandal M.Sc.

Size of Firm: 10–50 people
Works throughout Northern Ireland

Specialisation: Experience in large and small building projects; new build,
extensions & reconstructions
Design of stonework & timber structures
Interior designers & building surveyors

Background: Practice has 50 years experience in working with Historic
Buildings. Two of the partners worked for DOE Historic
Buildings Branch.
Donal MacRandal completed RSUA/QUB Certificate in
Architectural Conservation and Dermot MacRandal is a part-time
lecturer in History of Architecture at QUB

Membership: RIBA, FRIAI, Associate of the Chartered Institute of Arbitrators,
Fellow of the Institute of Management

Examples of Work: 1998
(L) Rademon, 1st Kilmore Non Subscribing Presbyterian Church,
Co. Down
Complete restoration of Grade A listed building

1998
(L) Clonard Monastery, Clonard Gardens, Belfast
Restoration and renovation to comply with current Safety/Fire
standards

1998
(L) Tower House, Co. Galway
Restoration of 15th century semi-ruined tower house to a single
family dwelling, using original technology and materials

1998
(L) Cave House, Cushendun
Extensive refurbishment of a substantial residence within the
Conservation Area

UAHS ref no. 41

Also: Consultant – Building Surveyor, Planning Supervisor, Interior Designer

Consultant – ARCHITECT

Manor Architects
Stable Buildings, Manor House
30a High Street
Moneymore
Co. Londonderry BT45 7PD

Telephone: 016487 48367   **Fax:** 016487 48579

Contact: Keith Gilmour

Size of Firm: 1–10 people
Works throughout Northern Ireland

Specialisation: Restoration, conservation and extension of traditional buildings, with knowledge of local craftspeople and materials
Currently setting up a library of traditional materials eg, joinery, slates, stone, sash windows and proposes to open up local kilns for production of lime putty

Background: 21 years as chartered architect in private practice, attended DoE/UAHS lime course 1993, staff participation in RSUA/QUB conservation course 1998

Membership: RIBA, RSUA, UAHS, ARBUK

Examples of Work: ongoing
(L) Erganagh Rectory, Omagh
Restoration of former rectory and conversion to private dwelling house

1996
(M) Bellaghy Bawn, Bellaghy
Complete renovation of the plantation house to form a visitors' centre including the Seamus Heaney Collection, for DoE Historic Monuments

1996
(L) 38/40 Main Street, Toomebridge
Restoration to provide retail outlet and living accommodation above

1993
(L) Assembly Rooms, Moneymore
Renovation & extension using local limestone & lime mortar

UAHS ref no. 43

Consultant – ARCHITECT

Roger McMichael Architect
2A High Street
Holywood
Co. Down BT18 9AZ

Telephone: 01232 428363 **Fax:** 01232 422151

Contact: Roger McMichael

Size of Firm: 1–10 people
Works throughout Northern Ireland

Background: Partner in multi-disciplinary practice 1974–1991
Principal in private practice 1991 to present

Membership: RIBA, RIAI

Examples of Work: (L) Pearl Assurance House, Donegal Square East, Belfast
Internal refurbishment
Architect: Roger McMichael

(L) Imperial House, Donegall Square East, Belfast
Replacement of facade
Architect: Roger McMichael

(L) 24 Shore Road, Holywood
Refurbishment
Architect: Roger McMichael

UAHS ref no. 542

Consultant – ARCHITECT

O'Hagan & Associates Architects
7 Trevor Hill
Newry
Co. Down

Telephone: 01693 66011   **Fax:** 01693 60904

Contact: Patrick O'Hagan

Size of Firm: 1–10 people
Works throughout Ireland

Specialisation: Architects and interior designers

Background: The practice has 13 years experience in dealing with listed buildings and buildings within Conservation Areas. The practice received two awards from the Prince's Trust and Newry Regeneration Project administered by the Department of the Environment

Membership: RIBA, RSUA

Examples of Work: 1998
(L) St John's Church, Hilltown
Major renovations to existing church

1998
(L) Dromantine College, Jerretz Pass, Co. Down
Comprehensive renovations and refurbishment to existing building

1994
(L) Downshire Arms, Hilltown
Major renovation to existing building and conversion of out-building to flats

1992
(L) Martray House, Ballygawley
Completed renovations to dwelling and courtyard buildings

UAHS ref no. 406

Consultant– ARCHITECT

Richard H Pierce
30 Paget Lane
Enniskillen
Co. Fermanagh BT74 7HS
Telephone: 01365 326630 / 323099   **Fax:** 01365 325186

Contact: Richard H Pierce RIBA

Size of Firm: 1–10 people
Works throughout Northern Ireland and the Republic of Ireland

Specialisation: Restoration & conservation work of buildings in architecturally
sensitive areas

Background: Richard Pierce has practised architecture over the past 30 years,
the last 20 of which have been in his own private practice

Membership: RIBA

Examples of Work: 1990
(L) Buttermarket, Enniskillen
Complete renovation of old Buttermarket to form craft & design
centre

1991
(L) Castlebarracks, Enniskillen
History & heritage centre

1996
(L) Belle Isle Estate, Lisbellaw, Co. Fermanagh
Restoration of courtyard

1997
Carlow Cathedral, Co. Carlow
Restoration and re-ordering of the fabric

1997
(L) St Macartan's Cathedral, Enniskillen
Restoration following devastating fire

UAHS ref no. 53

Consultant – ARCHITECT

Denis Piggot Architect
78 Drumnaconagher Road,
Crossgar
Co. Down BT30 9JH

Telephone: 01396 830800 **Fax:** 01396 830800

Contact: Denis Piggot

Size of Firm: 2 people
Works throughout Northern Ireland

Specialisation: Conservation architect – specialising in restoration work since starting own practice in 1984, with particular interest in vernacular buildings, industrial archaeology, & wind & water mills
Former Part-time Inspector for Environment Service – Historic Monuments & Buildings, listing buildings & inspecting work on site
Interested in new build in the traditional styles

Background: Attended SPAB course for architects & builders in 1986 and RSUA Conservation Course 1998
Has carried out over thirty restoration projects for the National Trust, together with wide range of projects for private clients on domestic, commercial & farm buildings. Has worked on over 50 listed buildings
Won awards in 1988 DoE competitions, 'Design a house in the countryside' & 'Houses in harmony'
Assisted the DoE in preparation of two Conservation Area design guides

Membership: RIBA, RSUA, committee of Hearth Housing Association, SPAB, NT, UAHS, member of Lecale Building Preservation Trust

Examples of Work: 1991
(L) Springhill Estate, Moneymore
Restoration of 17th century barn & other buildings including the dove cote

1992
(L) Castle Ward Estate, Strangford
Restoration of the cornmill & ancillary buildings

1993
(L) Private country house, Banbridge
Comprehensive restoration of neglected Georgian country house

UAHS ref no. 54

1996
(L) Denvir's Hotel, Downpatrick
Major scheme of repairs & refurbishment – in Downpatrick Conservation Area

Consultant – ARCHITECT

R Robinson & Sons
'Albany Villas'
59 High Street
Ballymoney
Co. Antrim BT53 6BG

Telephone: 012656 62127   **Fax:** 012656 66027

Contact: Richard Hunter

Size of Firm: 10–50 people
Works throughout Northern Ireland

Specialisation: Practice was established in 1924 & undertakes all types of commissions, specialising in the refurbishment of listed buildings & the preparation of condition reports, particularly for ecclesiastical buildings.

Background: Consultants to the National Trust
Architects to the Route Presbytery

Membership: RIBA, ARICS, MICE, MCIWEM

Examples of Work: 1992
(L) Mount Stewart, Greyabbey, Co. Down
Re-roofing, replacement of leadwork, re-pointing & indenting stonework
Contract value £1 m

1992
(L) The Argory, Moy, Co. Tyrone
Re-roofing main house
Contract value £200,000

1994
(L) Church, Articlave, Castlerock
Re-roofing, removal of external walling & re-building, re-leading & updating leaded windows
Contract value £200,000

1993
(L) The Argory, Moy, Co. Tyrone
Conversion of barn to education centre
Contract value £150, 000

UAHS ref no. 56

Consultant – ARCHITECT

Harry Rolston Chartered Architect
616 Upper Newtownards Road
Stormont
Belfast BT4 3HG

Telephone: 01232 657731   **Fax:** 01232 591474
E-mail: rolston@rchitect.dnet.co.uk   **Mobile:** 0802 350093

Contact: Harry Rolston

Size of Firm: 1–10 people
Works throughout Ireland & UK

Specialisation: New build – residential, commercial, recreational & industrial
Conservation, restoration & repairs to listed, historic &
ecclesiastical buildings & monuments
Adaptation, refurbishment & extensions to historic buildings
Condition surveys, studies & reports on historic buildings
Feasibility studies & cost plans
Computer aided design / drafting surveys & archiving
Project / building / maintenance management
Health & safety (CDM) services

Background: Chartered architectural practice
Consultants to the National Trust
Conservation Architect

Membership: ARCUK, RIBA, RSUA, MRIAI, MAPS, UAHS, NT

Examples of Work: 1994 – ongoing
(L) Computer aided design & drafting surveys of National Trust
properties throughout Northern Ireland
Castle Coole & Mount Stewart completed

ongoing
(L) Kearney Village, Co. Down
Conversion & refurbishment of stone buildings, for the National
Trust

1996
(L) The Argory, Moy
Stonework repairs, installation of new services & refurbishment
of windows & doors, for the National Trust

1995
(L) Rowallane House, Saintfield
Internal refurbishment & extension, for the National Trust

UAHS ref no. 44

40

Consultant – ARCHITECT

Shaffrey Associates
29 Lower Ormond Quay
Dublin 1

Telephone: 00 353 1 8725602   **Fax:** 00 353 1 8725614
                                  E-mail: shaffreyassoc.@dubi.ie

Contact: Patrick Shaffrey or Grainne Shaffrey

Size of Firm: 1–10 people
Work to date has been in the Republic of Ireland

Specialisation: All aspects of architectural conservation & restoration
Knowledge & understanding of traditional materials
Town & village design & renewal

Background: Over thirty years' experience in architectural conservation and
urban design & renewal

Membership: FRIAI, MRTPI, IPI, IOHBC, IPCRA

Examples of Work: 1994
(L) King House, Boyle, Co. Roscommon
Comprehensive restoration of large & historically important
house which had lain in derelict condition
Winner of RIAI Regional Award 1995

1994 – ongoing
(L) Ardfert Cathedral, Ardfert, Co. Kerry
Restoration / conservation of the south transept of St Brendan's
Cathedral, a 12th – 15th century Medieval building

1996
Cavan County Museum, Ballyjamesduff, Co. Cavan
Conversion of 19th century convent to new county museum

1997
(L) Wicklow Head Lighthouse, Wicklow
Restoration of 18th century granite structure as holiday
accommodation for the Irish Landmark Trust

UAHS ref no. 176

Also: Consultant – Urban Design & Town Planning,
Historic & Traditional Buildings Consultant

Consultant – ARCHITECT

Peter Shaw Chartered Architects
3 Deanfield
Londonderry BT47 6HY

Telephone: 01504 342501 **Fax:** 01504 342501

Contact: P G M Shaw DA (Edin.) RIBA, MRIAI

Size of Firm: 1–10 people
Works throughout Northern Ireland

Specialisation: Architectural restoration with a particular interest in the restoration of stonework & stained glass

Membership: RIBA, RIAI, SPAB

Examples of Work: 1998
(L) St Augustine's Parish Church, Londonderry
External refurbishment

1998
(L) First Derry Presbyterian Church, Londonderry
External refurbishment

1998
(L) Greevagh House, Londonderry
Roof replacement

1998
(L) Carricklee House Stable Yard, Strabane
Refurbishment

UAHS ref no. 59

Consultant – ARCHITECT

Smith & Fay Architects, Planners & Designers
22 Kilmorey Street
Newry
Co. Down BT34 2DE

Telephone: 01693 67311   **Fax:** 01693 252311

Contact: Gerald Fay

Size of Firm: 1–10 people
Works throughout Northern Ireland

Specialisation: Conservation, repair & restoration of listed buildings & vernacular buildings
Restoration of historic interiors
Conservation Area consultancy
Surveys, reports & feasibility studies

Background: 37 years in practice
Architectural advisor to the DoE for the Conservation Areas in Newry, Bessbrook & Rostrevor
Consultant / authors of the Newry Conservation Area book (DoE 1992)
Member of Historic Buildings Council NI 1988–1994

Membership: RIBA, RSUA

Examples of Work: 1986
(L) Kilbroney House, Rostrevor

1987
(L) Abbey Buildings, Newry
Recipient of Times / RIBA Award

1992
(L) Town Hall, Newry
Centenary restoration

1993
(L) Church, Cooley

UAHS ref no. 341

Also: Consultant – Urban Design & Town Planning, Architectural Historian, Interior Designer

Consultant – ARCHITECT

	Larry Thompson Partnership
	Architects
	4 Kinegar Avenue
	Holywood BT18 9JR
Telephone:	01232 422986
Contact:	Larry Thompson
Size of Firm:	1–10 people
	Works throughout Northern Ireland
Specialisation:	Conversion of old buildings to modern use
	Repairs & refurbishment of existing buildings
	Design guides for the Department of the Environment
Background:	Assessors 1992 – 1995 for Europa Nostra Awards for NI
	Diploma of Architecture – Edinburgh
Membership:	RIBA, past President – RSUA

Examples of Work:

1993
Ballygally, Co. Antrim
Alterations, additions & refurbishment of an existing traditional farmhouse for an artist / university tutor, incorporating an artist's studio

1994
The Quay, Dundrum
Conversion of stone built locomotive shop to four apartment dwellings

1994
The Buck's Head Restaurant, Main Street, Dundrum
Repairs, alterations & extension to existing stone built building, inc. major refurbishment of interior

1995
(L) Bridge House, Carnalea
Work to main roof, eradicating dry-rot, internal refurbishment

UAHS ref no. 181

Consultant – ARCHITECT

Twenty-Two Over Seven
The Ormeau Baths
Ormeau Avenue
Belfast BT2 8HS

Telephone: 01232 322726   **Fax:** 01232 249520

Contact: Doug Elliott

Size of Firm: 1–10 people
Works throughout Northern Ireland

Specialisation: Architecture & design
Conservation of listed buildings; restoration & conversion of redundant buildings for new uses; & sympathetic new building extensions to listed buildings
Urban renewal; new buildings; innovative modern interventions; & interiors

Membership: RSUA, RIBA, ARCUK

Examples of Work: ongoing
(L) former Belfast Gas Works
Restoration & conversion for new use of major group of listed, industrial buildings, together with new buildings on vacant land
Contract value £5 m

ongoing
(L) Coastal Centre, Killough, Co. Down
Repair & conversion of an 18th/19th century grain store, adjacent stables and coach house, to provide a new coastal centre and community museum

1992–1997
(L) The Ormeau Baths, Belfast
Restoration & refurbishment of original Victorian public baths for re-use as public art gallery & office accommodation
Contract value £2 m
RSUA Award 1998 Urban Regeneration, RSUA Commendation 1998 Tourism & Leisure, Healthy Building of the Year Award 1994

1996
(L) The Queen's University of Belfast
Visitors' centre within the Lanyon Building including provision for shop & exhibition facilities
Contract value £200,000

UAHS ref no. 451

Also: Consultant – Interior Designer – p. 50

45

Consultant – ARCHITECT

A & E Wright Architects and Designers
601 Lisburn Road
Belfast BT9 7GS

Telephone: 01232 667867   **Fax:** 01232 661146

Contact: Tony Wright or Elizabeth Wright

Size of Firm: 1–10 people
Works throughout Ireland

Specialisation: Conservation, restoration & adaption of Grade A listed buildings
Restoration of historic interiors
Leadwork, stonework, brickwork, slating, decorative plasterwork,
fine joinery, paintwork & other finishes
The provision of systems for environmental control, fire
prevention & security
Conservation plans
Condition surveys & reports on historic buildings
Feasibility studies & cost plans
Architectural historian, Garden landscape historian

Background: Architectural advisor to Planning Service for the Conservation
Areas in Ardglass, Downpatrick, Killough & Killyleagh
Architect to the National Trust

Membership: RIBA, HBC

Examples of Work: 1995
(L) Castle Coole, Co. Fermanagh

1997
(L) Temple of the Winds, Co. Down

1997
Hilden Primary School

ongoing
(L) Florencecourt, Co. Fermanagh

ongoing
Oakfield Park, Co. Donegal

UAHS ref no. 62

Also: Consultant – Architectural Historian, Garden / Landscape Historian,
Interior Designer, Historic & Traditional Buildings Consultant

Consultant – ARCHITECT

John McIlhagga RIBA Chartered Architect
105 Great Victoria Street
Belfast BT2 7AG

Telephone: 01232 320071   **Fax:** 01232 438222

Contact: John McIlhagga

Size of Firm: 1–10 people
Works throughout Northern Ireland

Specialisation: Consultancy services in connection with inspections, surveys and feasibility studies of listed and non-listed historic buildings
Preparation of information, schedules & specifications for clients on appropriate reinstatement & repairs
Re-use of redundant buildings
Preparation of maintenance programmes
Release of grant aid for approved building works

Background: Practice established in 1981
Clients include the National Trust; Environment & Heritage Service – Historic Buildings & Monuments; & the Department of the Environment – Planning Service

Membership: RIBA

UAHS ref no. 48

Consultant – ARCHITECTURAL

Garnet V Mills Architectural Consultant
203 Main Street
Lisnaskea
Co. Fermanagh BT92 OJH

Telephone: 01365 721574   **Fax:** 01365 721574

Contact: Garnet V Mills

Size of Firm: 1–10 people
Generally works in Fermanagh and south Tyrone

Specialisation: Restoration of historic buildings

Background: 13 years as a technician in an architect's practice and 25 years in own private practice

Membership: ACIoB

Examples of Work: 1996
(L) Crom, Newtownbutler
Repairs to slated roofs, leadwork & restoration of conservatory

1995
(L) Trinity Church, Derryvore, Derrylin
Repairs to slated roof, replacement of lead roof & valley, & repairs to dressed stonework

1996
(L) Gortineddan, Derrylin
Complete restoration & extension to traditional thatched cottage

1997
(L) Private country house at Sheebeg, Lisnaskea
Total restoration

UAHS ref no. 50

48

Consultant – CHARITY RESTORING HISTORIC BUILDINGS

Hearth
66 Donegall Pass
Belfast BT7 1BU

Telephone: 01232 530121 **Fax:** 01232 530122

Contact: Marcus Patton

Size of Firm: 1–10 people
Works throughout Northern Ireland

Specialisation: Restoration & conservation of listed buildings & buildings in Conservation Areas
Housing Association
Revolving Fund
Architectural practice

Background: Director: Architect, BSc., DipArch, RIBA
Staff also includes an architectural assistant

Membership: Hearth Revolving Fund is a member of the Association of Preservation Trusts
Hearth Housing Association is a member of the NI Federation of Housing Associations

Examples of Work: 1992
(L) Private houses, Castle Street / Upper Irish Street, Armagh
for Hearth Revolving Fund
Restoration of derelict Georgian houses & infill
Awarded a Europa Nostra Diploma in 1995

1994
(L) Houses & flats, 37–39 Court Street, Newtownards
for Hearth Housing Association
Conversion of stables & restoration of houses

1995
Traditional cottages, Co. Antrim
for Rural Cottage Holidays Ltd.
Restoration of six derelict cottages

1997
Alexandra Park, Belfast for Hearth Revolving Fund
Restoration of burnt out gate lodge

UAHS ref no. 30

See 'Hearth – A Review of Projects 1978–1993', Hearth, Belfast, 1994

Consultant – INTERIOR DESIGNER

Twenty-Two Over Seven
The Ormeau Baths
Ormeau Avenue
Belfast BT2 8HS

Telephone: 01232 322726   **Fax:** 01232 249520

Contact: Doug Elliott

Size of Firm: 1–10 people
Works throughout Northern Ireland

Specialisation: Architecture & design for industrial, commercial & domestic interiors
Conservation & reinterpretation of traditional interiors
Modern interventions within existing historic buildings & conversion for new uses, particularly office, gallery & exhibition space

Membership: RSUA, RIBA, ARCUK

Examples of Work: 1995
(L) Ormeau Baths Gallery, Ormeau Avenue, Belfast
Contemporary art gallery, extending over 10,000 sq. ft. – a modern intervention within the former Victorian public baths inc. restoration of original elements & new building works
RSUA Award 1998, Urban Regeneration
RSUA Commendation 1998, Tourism and Leisure

1992
(L) Private offices, Ormeau Baths
Fitting-out of former Victorian public baths, together with new building to provide 10,000 sq. ft. of office space
Healthy Building of the Year Award 1994

1996
(L) The Queen's University of Belfast
Visitors' centre within the Lanyon Building including provision for shop & exhibition facilities
Contract value £200,000

1994
(L) King Edward Building, Royal Victoria Hospital
Restoration & refurbishment of principal entrance to provide corporate reception suite
Contract value £60,000

UAHS ref no. 452

Also: Consultant – Architect – p. 45

Consultant – ARCHITECT

Ferguson & McIlveen – p. 67
G M Design Associates – p. 68

Consultant – INTERIOR DESIGNER

Ferguson & McIlveen – p. 67
G M Design Associates – p. 68
MacRandal Partnership – p. 33
McCutcheon & Wilkinson – p. 30
Smith & Fay – p. 43
A & E Wright – p. 46

Consultant – PLANNING SUPERVISOR & PROJECT MANAGEMENT

Consarc Design Group – p. 65
Isherwood & Ellis – p. 21
MacRandal Partnership – p. 33

Consultant – HISTORIC & TRADITIONAL BUILDING CONSULTANCY & TRAINING

Narrow Water Lime Service
Newry Road
Warrenpoint
Co. Down BT34 3LE

Telephone: 016937 53073   **Fax:** 016937 53073

Contact: Dan McPolin

Size of Firm: 1–10 people
Works throughout Northern Ireland

Specialisation: Consultancy service offering advice on the use of traditional materials for the repair of historic buildings
Analysis of lime mortars & renders
'Lime Workshops' – demonstrations & hands on, practical courses in the preparation & use of traditional lime putty (limestone burned & slaked on site) for building & pointing mortars, renders, harls, fine plasters & limewashes

Background: Time served plasterer
Housing Inspector, Dept. of the Environment
Superintendent of works for Historic Monuments & Buildings Branch of the DoE, from 1985 to 1995
Founded Narrow Water Lime Service in July 1995

Membership: Building Limes Forum, Institute of Clerks of Works, SPAB

Examples of work: Mortar analysis & preparation of new lime mortars for external repairs & re-rendering / harling to private houses at:

1996
Ballynahinch
Architect: Hobart & Heron, Holywood

1996
(L) Banbridge
Architect: Denis Piggot, Crossgar

1996
(L) Magherlin
Supervising Officer: Dan McPolin

ongoing
(L) Dundonald
Supervising Officer: Dan McPolin

UAHS ref no. 445

Also: Sub-Contractor – Stone, Brick, Plasterwork (Lime Plasters & Renders)
Supplier – Lime Putty, Mortars & Limewashes – p. 184

52

ARCHITECTURAL HISTORIAN

Sophia Chambre
1 Fairview
Saintfield
Co. Down

Telephone: 01238 511159   **e-mail:** sgc.svc@dnet.co.uk

Contact: Sophia Chambre

Size of Firm: Works throughout Ireland

Specialisation: Architectural historian

Background: Currently undertaking a PhD on the architecture of the Irish Country House 1790–1840

Membership: UAHS, Society of Architectural Historians, Irish Georgian Society, Georgian Society

Examples of Work: ongoing
(L) Ballynatray, Co. Waterford
Historical survey of house & demesne

1997
(L) Lissadell, Co. Sligo
MA thesis. The Country House in Architectural Discourse

ongoing
(L) National Trust, Northern Ireland Region
updating vernacular buildings survey

Sub-Contractor – GARDEN/LANDSCAPE HISTORIAN

Belinda Jupp, Garden Historian
42 Osborne Park
Belfast BT9 6JN

Telephone: 01232 668817   **Fax:** 01232 666506

Size of Firm: 1 person
Works throughout UK and Republic of Ireland

Specialisation: Garden Historian: the conservation and restoration of historic gardens including historic landscape survey: restoration plans: planting plans: supervision of restoration

Background: Graduate diploma in Garden Conservation, Architectural Association, London
City & Guilds: Horticulture

Examples of Work: DoE (NI)
Compiled inventory of historic parks, gardens and demesnes: subsequently a Register of selected sites to be added to local authority Area Plans

1998
Antrim Castle Gardens, Co. Antrim
Historic landscape survey for Heritage Lottery Funding application
Gordon and Woburn Squares, London

Historic Landscape survey for Great Gardens of Ireland Restoration Programme
Belvedere, Co. Westmeath (with T McErlean & T Reeves-Smith) historic demesne survey with recommendations for restoration

ongoing
Kylemore Abbey, Co. Galway
Restoration of Victorian walled garden: site survey (plants): recommendations for restoration: planting plans: supervision of project

UAHS ref no. 525

54

Consultant – GARDEN/LANDSCAPE HISTORIAN

Thomas McErlean
53 Camden Street
Belfast BT9 6AT

Telephone: 01232 23136

Contact: Thomas McErlean

Size of Firm: 1
Works throughout Ireland

Specialisation: Garden Archaeologist: the supervision, conservation and restoration of parks and gardens including excavation and historic landscape surveys

Background: Graduate archaeologist

Examples of Work: projects to date
Great Gardens of Ireland Restoration Programme (consultant)
Restoration Projects and Historic Landscape Surveys include;
Kylemore Abbey, Co. Galway; Turlough and Enniscoe, Co. Mayo; Woodstock, Co. Kilkenny
Castle Coole; Castleward; Antrim Castle Gardens; Birr Castle Gardens, Co. Offaly; Marley Park, Co. Dublin; Belvedere, Co. Westmeath

UAHS ref no. 569

55

Consultant – ENVIRONMENTAL CONSULTANT

Spouncer Associates
Environmental Management
45 St Patrick's Avenue
Downpatrick
Co. Down BT30 6DN

Telephone: 01396 616066   **Fax:** 01396 616066

Contact: Celia Spouncer

Size of Firm: 1–10 people
Works throughout Ireland

Specialisation: A small-scale, locally based consultancy offering advice, training & facilitation in environmental projects; community landscapes; landscape management & design; integrating 'environment' into economic & rural development projects & networking with wide range of professionals in green buildings; energy efficiency; renewable energy; waste management & recycling

Background: MSc. Landscape Ecology, Design & Maintenance
Registered landscape practice & registered environmental auditor
Experience with governmental, public & private organisations in ecological & landscape assessment, landscape planning, environmental management & interpretation

Membership: Landscape Institute, associate of Institute of Ecology & Management, associate of Environmental Auditors Registration Association

Examples of Work: Mournes Environment & Visitor Management Strategy
Lower Bann Recreation & Tourism Strategy
Woodland Study on Rathlin

'Local Agenda 21' report for Northern Ireland Environment Link & the World Wildlife Fund

Training for volunteers & community leaders in opportunities for environmental projects

Design of school landscapes for environmental education, & design of wildlife areas

UAHS ref no. 333

Consultant – ARCHITECTURAL HISTORIAN

Consultant – GARDEN / LANDSCAPE HISTORIAN

Consultant – HISTORIC & TRADITIONAL BUILDINGS

Consultant – LANDSCAPE ARCHITECT

Consultant – ENVIRONMENTAL CONSULTANT

Consultant – URBAN DESIGN & TOWN PLANNING

Consultant – PHOTOGRAPHER

Consultant – ANALYSIS & SPECIFICATION OF STONE & RELATED MATERIALS

Lithan Ltd.
5B Ards Business Centre
Newtownards
Co. Down BT23 4YH
Telephone: 01247 819787 ext. 221   **Fax:** 01247 820625

Contact: John Kelly

Size of Firm: 1–10 people
Works throughout Ireland

Specialisation: Analysis of stone alterations & evaluation of intervention procedures & materials
Analysis of bronzework & evaluation of intervention procedures & materials
Project specification & supervision

Background: Senior conservator, Ulster Museum
Geology degree, QUB

Membership: IPCRA, ICOMOS, ICHAW, UKIC, MGC Conservation Register

Examples of Work: (L) Church, Donegall Street, Belfast
Evaluation of treatments & mortars; preparation of specifications & supervision

(L) Cathedral, Armagh
Analysis & evaluation of treatments & stone
Architect: Leighton Johnston Associates, Belfast

1996
(L) 2 Royal Avenue, Belfast (Tesco Metro supermarket)
Analysis, specification and implementation of work to remove paint, restore stonework & re-paint external envelope

1996
(L) Town Hall, Enniskillen
Analysis, specification and implementation of cleaning, repair & restoration of stonework & leadwork, for Fermanagh District Council

UAHS ref no. 398

Also: Sub-Contractor – Stone – p. 97, Monumental Bronze

Consultant – BUILDING SURVEYOR

Hunter Associates
Chartered Architects & Building Surveyors
19A High Street
Ballymoney BT53 6AH

Telephone: 012656 63535   **Fax:** 012656 63535

Contact: James Morrison

Size of Firm: 1–10 people
Works throughout Northern Ireland

Specialisation: Restoration and reconstruction of listed buildings & churches
Inspections & surveys
Preparation of reports & schedules of conditions

Background: 20 years' experience of working on refurbishment &
reconstruction, clients in the public & private sectors
Work extensively in Conservation Areas

Membership: Chartered building surveyor, RICS

Examples of Work: 1993
(L) Lissanoure Castle Visitors' Centre, Loughguile, Ballymoney
To convert former byre & stables to public house with catering &
function room facilities

1997
(L) 30 Springbank Road, Downhill
Restructuring of thatched cottage

1998
45 Main Street, Ballymoney
Replacement of shop front to match the original

ongoing
(L) 9 Leslie Hill, Ballymoney
Rebuilding of east pavilion wing to main house

UAHS ref no. 177

Consultant – QUANTITY SURVEYOR

David Gould Associates
Chartered Quantity Surveyors & Construction Consultants
62 Lisburn Road
Belfast BT7 1NR

Telephone: 01232 320050   **Fax:** 01232 333899

Contact: David Gould

Size of Firm: 1–10 people
Works throughout Northern Ireland

Specialisation: Construction & contract advice; tender procurement
Feasibility studies
Cost planning; Planning Supervisor

Background: D Gould – trained at Thames Polytechnic, London
Surveyors in the practice are qualified by the Royal Institution of
Chartered Surveyors

Membership: RICS

Examples of Work: 1998
(L) Convent, Rossmore Drive, Belfast
Conversion of Convent into 40 flats
Architect: Lyons Architects, Belfast

1996
(L) Down Hunt Club, English Street, Downpatrick
Conversion to restaurant – in Downpatrick Conservation Area
Architect: M D Architects, Belfast

1994
Heritage Centre, Church Bay, Rathlin Island
Conversion of derelict boathouse to Heritage Centre
Landscape Architect: S Visick, Belfast

1994
(L) Church Street, Antrim
Alterations & extensions to church

UAHS ref no. 66

Consultant – STRUCTURAL ENGINEER

Brian C Campbell
38 Mill Street
Ballymena
Co. Antrim BT43 5AE

Telephone: 01266 653759   **Fax:** 01266 47326

Contact: Brian Campbell

Size of Firm: 1–10 people
Works throughout Ireland

Specialisation: Structural assessments of buildings and monuments
Preparation of design and details for remedial work and/or
alterations to existing structures

Background: Chartered structural engineer for over 25 years
Own practice since 1980

Membership: I.C.E., I.S.E., Concrete Society, Timber Research & Development
Association

Examples of Work: 1997
(L) St Patrick's Church, Ballymena
Restoration of the fabric, including replacement of stone tracery
and re-installation of stained glass in an isothermal manner
Architect: Brian Campbell, Ballymena

1996
11 Vicar's Hill, Armagh
(L) Underpinning and stabilising of gable walling
Architect: Leighton Johnston Associates

1995
(L) National Museum of Ireland, Collin's Barracks, Dublin
Structural ties to stabilise masonry walls
Architect: Lee McCullough & Partners

1993
(L) Old Waterside Hospital, Fever Block, Londonderry
Change of use to offices, as well as extension following partial
demolition
Architect: State Services Directorate

UAHS ref no. 560

Consultant – STRUCTURAL ENGINEER

W J McDowell McGladdery & Partners
Aldersgate House
13–19 University Road
Belfast BT7 1NA

Telephone: 01232 245444 **Fax:** 01232 245916

Contact: Bill Montgomery, Adrian Erskine

Size of Firm: 10–50 people
Works throughout Northern Ireland

Specialisation: Structural assessment of historic and traditional buildings and structures, including preparation of reports and recommendations
Structural restoration of deteriorating concrete buildings and structures.
Structural design and supervision on site of new building works.
Planning supervisor

Background: Chartered Structural engineers with over 25 years experience including work on many National Trust properties
Recipient of 1986 Civic Trust Award for work in connection with restoration of Annalong Cornmill

Membership: ACE, FIEI, FISE

Examples of Work: 1992
(L) Town Hall, Portadown
Structural restoration & conversion of 19th century building
Architect: Maurice Cushnie

1994
(L) Town Hall, Newry
Major scheme of internal alterations
Architect: Smith & Fay, Newry

1995
(L) Castlecoole, Co. Fermanagh
Restoration of building fabric
Architect: A & E Wright, Belfast

1998
(L) Denvir's Hotel, Downpatrick
Structural restoration & extension of 17th century buildings in conservation area
Architect: Denis Piggot, Crossgar

UAHS ref no. 73

Consultant – BUILDING SERVICES ENGINEER

Beattie Flanigan & Partners
174 Castlereagh Road
Belfast BT5 5GX

Telephone: 01232 732121   **Fax:** 01232 732630

Contact: Harry Flanigan

Size of Firm: 10–50 people
Works throughout Northern Ireland

Specialisation: Building Services Consulting Engineering Practice carrying out design of M & E installations in all types of buildings, selection of suitable contractors, site supervision & contract management. Collaboration with other building professionals on the integration of M & E services into existing historic buildings inc. work with the National Trust

Background: Partnership formed in April 1971

Membership: IMechE, IEE, CIBSE, ACE

Examples of Work: 1991
(L) Castle Ward, Strangford
Selective refurbishment of M & E services in main Mansion House & provision of new services to exhibition & visitor facilities
Architect: Hearth, Belfast

1992
(L) Public Building, Belfast
Major refurbishment of heating, ventilation, air-conditioning & electrical installations
Architect: Consarc Design Group Ltd., Belfast

1993
(L) SELB Offices, The Mall, Armagh
Major refurbishment of heating, plumbing & electrical services installations in Georgian terraced buildings
Architect: SELB Architects Department

1994
(L) Downshire Arms Hotel, Hilltown
Major refurbishment of heating, ventilation, plumbing & electrical services installations in main hotel & chalets
Architect: Patrick O'Hagan & Associates, Newry

UAHS ref no. 75

63

Consultant – BUILDING SURVEYOR

Consarc Design Group – p. 65
V B Evans & Company – p. 66
Isherwood & Ellis – p. 18
MacRandal Partnership – p. 30
O'Neill Bros. (Building Contractors) Ltd. – p. 129

Consultant – QUANTITY SURVEYOR

Consarc Design Group – p. 65
V B Evans & Company – p. 66
Global Stone Company Ltd. – p. 95
O'Neill Bros. (Building Contractors) Ltd. – p. 129

Consultant – STRUCTURAL & CIVIL ENGINEERS

V B Evans & Company – p. 66
Ferguson McIlveen – p. 67
McCutcheon & Wilkinson – p. 68

Consultant – MULTI-DISCIPLINARY CONSULTANCY

Consarc Design Group Ltd.
50 Stranmillis Embankment
Belfast BT9 5FL

Telephone: 01232 381711 **Fax:** 01232 381688

Contact: Tony Stevens, Billy Mol or Noel Graham

Size of Firm: 35–50 people
Works throughout Ireland

Specialisation: Architecture
Building surveying
Quantity surveying
Project management
Practice incorporates Consarc Conservation, specialist
architectural conservation service (see entry under Consultant –
Architect)

Background: Fully qualified architects, quantity surveyors & project managers
Practice formed in 1911

Membership: RIBA, RIAI, RICS, IOHBC

Examples of Work: 1993
(L) Comgall House, Holywood
Full restoration & extensions for Glencraig School

1995
(L) St James's Street, London
Structural repairs & restoration of Thomas Hopper designed
interior of 1827 inc. plasterwork, joinery & faux marble
decoration

1996
(L) Ulster Print Works, Newtownards
Restoration of stone building with new housing in grounds

1997
The Foyer, Malone Road, Belfast
(L) Restoration of building & major extension for hostel
accommodation

UAHS ref no. 9

Also: Consultant – Architect – p. 7, Project Management

Consultant – MULTI-DISCIPLINARY CONSULTANCY

V B Evans & Company
19 College Gardens
Belfast BT9 6BP

Telephone: 01232 381211   **Fax:** 01232 661353

Contact: David W Allen FRICS

Size of Firm: 10–50 people
Works throughout Northern Ireland & England

Specialisation: Quantity Surveying
Building Surveying
Structural Surveys
Assistance with grant applications
Insurance Valuations

Background: Staff are trained, experienced & qualified in each of the above disciplines & specialist areas of expertise

Membership: Company contains Fellows and Associates of the RICS, a Chartered Engineer & Member of the Institution of Civil Engineering

Examples of Work: ongoing from 1994
(L) Public school, Belfast
General repair work to building envelope inc. stone & leadwork, rainwater goods & roofs

1998
(L) Public building, N.W. England
Re-roofing, stonework repairs & dry rot treatment

1996
(L) Church building, Belfast
Survey, report & repairs to slating & leadwork

1996
(L) Temple of the Winds, Mount Stewart
Replacement of the roof, repairs to defective stonework, restoration of decorative plasterwork, & environmental heating

UAHS ref no. 65

Offices also at 2 Lodge Road, Coleraine, tel. 01265 44457
Also: Structural & Civil Engineer, Building Surveyor, Quantity Surveyor

Consultant – MULTI-DISCIPLINARY CONSULTANCY

Ferguson & McIlveen
Beechill House
Beechill Road
Belfast BT8 4RP

Telephone: 01232 705111 **Fax:** 01232 795651

Contact: John Baird

Size of Firm: 50+
Works throughout Northern Ireland and Great Britain

Specialisation: Architecture & interior design
Civil & structural engineering
Landscape architecture & environmental consultancy
Specialists skills include structural facing repair, structural steel repair, stained glass windows, restoration of original external plasterwork & roofing

Background: Many years' experience of building restoration projects inc. banks, churches, houses & railway stations

Membership: RIBA, ACA, ACE, ICE, ISE, IEI, LI, RTPI, IEA, MIWEM, IHT

Examples of Work: 1992
(L) Private offices, Clarendon Dock, Belfast
Major scheme of restoration & refurbishment
Recipient of Europa Nostra Award 1994

1992
(L) Educational building, Belfast
Internal refurbishment & conservation of original Neo-Georgian detailing

(L) Former warehouses, Victoria Street, Belfast
Feasibility study for the restoration of redundant Grade A listed warehouses

1993
Church, Bangor
Reinstatement of building after bomb damage

UAHS ref no. 21

Also: Consultant – Architect, Structural & Civil Engineer, Landscape Architect, Environmental Consultant, Interior Designer

Consultant – MULTI-DISCIPLINARY CONSULTANCY

G M Design Associates
22 Lodge Road
Coleraine
Co. Londonderry BT52 1NB

Telephone: 01265 56138   **Fax:** 01265 42699

Contact: Bill Gamble or Kieran Mullan

Size of Firm: 10–50 people
Works throughout Northern Ireland

Specialisation: Architecture
Urban conservation & town planning
Interior Design

Background: Practice partners and staff are all fully qualified in their own field

Membership: RIBA, RTPI

Examples of Work: 1993
(L) Galgorm Manor, Ballymena
Major scheme of refurbishment & alterations, comprehensive
internal redecoration & new function suite

1993/4
(L) Private houses, Castleroe Road, Coleraine
Restoration and refurbishment of semi-derelict, former estate
stables and outhouses to form townhouses and apartments in
mews complex

1997
(L) Private offices, 24 Lodge Road, Coleraine
Refurbishment & extension to existing building

ongoing
(L) Yorkshire House, Belfast
Restoration and refurbishment of office building to form hotel,
including restaurants etc.

UAHS ref no. 22

Also: Consultant – Architect, Urban Design & Town Planning, Interior Designer

Consultant – MULTI-DISCIPLINARY CONSULTANCY

McCutcheon & Wilkinson – p. 27

MAIN CONTRACTOR

Jose Alves-Areias Building Contractor
10 Ethel Street
Belfast BT9 7FW

Telephone: 01232 663483 **Fax:** 01232 663483

Contact: Jose Alves-Areias

Size of Firm: 1–10 people
Works in Belfast & within a radius of 20 miles

Specialisation: Slating & roofing
Brickwork
Leadwork
Joinery
Plasterwork
Tiles & tiling

Background: In the building trade for the last 34 years

Membership: Federation of Master Builders

Examples of Work: (L) Private house, Killyleagh
Repairs to stonework, bay roof, chimney & lead valleys
Architect: A Coey, Belfast

1997
Private house, Windsor Park, Belfast
Conversion into 5 flats

ongoing
(L) Gate Lodge, Sydenham Avenue, Belfast
Extension of listed gatelodge to office accommodation
Architect: A Coey, Belfast

ongoing
(L) Ardara House, Comber
Renewal of guttering and external works on large mansion
recently converted into flats

UAHS ref no. 76

*Also: Sub-Contractor – Slating & Roofing, Brick, Leadwork, Joinery, Plasterwork,
Tiles and Tiling
Services & Utilities – Electrician, Plumber*

MAIN CONTRACTOR

Building Services
49 Bessbrook Road
Tullyallen
Mountnorris
Co. Armagh BT60 2DD

Telephone: 01861 507576   **Fax:** 01861 507576

Contact: Noel Cochrane

Size of Firm: 1–10 people
Works in counties Down & Armagh

Specialisation: Traditional building work, inc. internal joinery, plasterwork repairs & *in situ* run mouldings, repairs & draught proofing of sash windows, structural timber repairs & remedial works, and new build to traditional standards and styles

Background: Family business for 35 years, Noel Cochrane has 16 years' experience in all aspects of building work

Membership: Guild of Master Craftsmen, Roof Force, NHBC approved and registered contractor. Warranted contractor for NIHE grant works

Examples of Work: 1994
Private house, Newry
Renovation of dwelling inc. repairs to roof structure, new chimneys, flue linings & cast iron gutters, repairs to leadwork & re-roofing in reclaimed slate

1993
Former stable block, Newry
Extensive repairs & replacement of damaged roof structure, treatment of rot & re-slating of roof in reclaimed & new slate

1996
Private house, Bessbrook
Structural repairs to roof timbers & re-roofing, new leadwork, replacement of damaged internal & external joinery with reclaimed pitch pine, repairs to sliding sash windows & installation of draught proofing system

1996
Private house, Portadown
Conversion of out-buildings to form new bathroom & store inc. repairs to roof & new doors & windows
Supervising Officer: J W S Preston, Portadown

UAHS ref no. 413

Also: Sub-Contractor – Sash Windows – p. 133

MAIN CONTRACTOR

Patrick Campbell Building Contractor
40 Ballyvaddy Road
Carnlough
Ballymena
Co. Antrim BT44 0LG

Telephone: 01574 885333

Contact: Patrick Campbell

Size of Firm: 1–10 people
Works throughout Northern Ireland

Specialisation: Slating & roofing
Plasterwork
Joinery

Background: Various building contracts including new private work,
renovations and work at the Ulster Folk and Transport Museum

Membership: Construction Industry Training Board

Examples of Work: 1990
Replica of Bank, Ulster Folk & Transport Museum
Construction of bank & manager's house
Supervising Officer: D Morris, UFTM, Cultra

1991
Replica of IOGT Hall, Ulster Folk & Transport Museum
Supervising Officer: D Morris, UFTM, Cultra

1992
Residential building, Ulster Folk & Transport Museum
Construction of terraced building to form residential
accommodation
Supervising Officer: D Morris, UFTM, Cultra

ongoing
Replica of Parochial Hall, Ulster Folk & Transport Museum
Supervising Officer: D Morris, UFTM, Cultra

UAHS ref no. 216

Also: Sub-Contractor – Slating & Roofing, Joinery, Plasterwork

MAIN CONTRACTOR

Castle Contracts
17 Castle Heights
Dundrum
Co. Down BT33 0RY

Telephone: 013967 51433   **Fax:** 013967 51433

Contact: Roy Connor & I Greene

Size of Firm: 10–50 people
Works in Ballyclare, Whitehead, Bangor, Lisburn, Newry & Belfast

Specialisation: Full supervision on all jobs using experienced craftsmen
All building, joinery, roofing, slating, leadwork, drainage & site work carried out by directly employed labour
Surveying services

Background: The owners are both joiners and have been general foremen with leading builders, each for 20 years

Membership: Building Guarantee Scheme NI

Examples of Work: (L) Church, Belmont, Belfast
Provision of fire prevention measures & means of escape, dry rot & roof repairs
Architect: Leighton Johnston Associates, Belfast

1992
Church Hall, Woodvale
Major scheme of restoration
Supervising Officer: BSB Building & Design, Belfast

1994
(L) Church, Whitehead
Re-pointing of main church & tower, replacement louvre windows & roof repairs
Architect: Gifford & Cairns, Belfast

1997
(L) Clock Tower, Castle Ward, Co. Down
Full restoration for the National Trust
Architect: Maurice Cushnie, Portadown

UAHS ref no. 274

Also: Sub-Contractor – Stone, Brick, Slating & Roofing, Joinery, Plasterwork, Tiles & Tiling, Painterwork, Remedial Works

MAIN CONTRACTOR

T Chambers & Sons (Enniskillen) Ltd.
58 Tempo Road
Enniskillen
Co. Fermanagh BT74 6HR

Telephone: 01365 322447   **Fax:** 01365 323882

Contact: Victor Chambers

Size of Firm: 10–50 people
Works throughout Northern Ireland

Specialisation: Stone restoration
Renders esp. lime & lime mortars
Joinery & carpentry
Leadwork

Background: Company has over 38 years experience in restoration work

Membership: Building Federation, Construction Industry Training Board

Examples of Work: 1995
(L) Visitors' centre, Crom, Co. Fermanagh
Restoration of cottages & visitors' centre, for the National Trust
Architect: J Neil Partnership, Belfast

1996
(L) Ulster Bank, Lisnaskea
Refurbished the whole building
Architect: McCarter, McGaw Architects, Dungannon

1997
(L) Clifton Lodge, Lisnaskea
Refurbished stonework on three storey building
Architect: Garnet V Mills, Lisnaskea

ongoing
(L) Crom Old Castle, Fermanagh
Rebuilding old walls
Architect: Garnet V Mills, Lisnaskea

UAHS ref no. 123

*Also: Sub-Contractor – Stone, Roofing & Slating, Leadwork, Joinery, Plasterwork,
Ironmongery, Painterwork*

MAIN CONTRACTOR

William Dowling Ltd.
71–73 Grand Street
Hilden
Lisburn BT27 4TX

Telephone: 01846 666444   **Fax:** 01846 629678

Contact: S Graham

Size of Firm: 10–50 people
Works throughout Northern Ireland

Specialisation: Main contractor
Joinery & joinery manufacturing
Shopfitting
Bricklaying & concreting
Plasterwork

Background: Many years' experience of renovating & repairing listed buildings

Membership: Construction Employers Federation

Examples of Work: (L) Public building, Belfast
Extensive refurbishment
Architect: Consarc Design Group Ltd., Belfast

(L) Private building, Belfast
Refurbishment, restoration of bomb damage & construction of
new portico
Architect: Consarc Design Group Ltd., Belfast

(L) Private offices, Belfast
Refurbishment of boardroom, ballroom & offices
Architect: R McKinstry, Lisburn

(L) Private offices, Belfast
Restoration, refurbishment & conversion of former harbour
buildings to form new offices
Architect: Ferguson & McIlveen, Belfast

UAHS ref no. 278

MAIN CONTRACTOR

J S Dunlop Building & Civil Engineering Contractor
Drumart, 48 Kirk Road
Ballymoney
Co. Antrim BT53 8HB

Telephone: 012656 63330   **Fax:** 012656 62742

Contact: Wallace Dunlop

Size of Firm: 10–50 people
Works in counties Antrim & Londonderry

Specialisation: General restoration works
Stonework replacement & repairs, repointing & stone walling
Specialist joinery
Natural slate roofing
Decorative plasterwork

Background: In business since 1969 with wide experience of traditional &
historic restorations for public & private clients inc. the National
Trust & Hearth Housing Association

Membership: Construction Employers Federation

Examples of Work: 1996 phase 1, 1997 phase 2
(L) Bishop's Palace, Downhill
Pointing stonework & stonework restoration
Architect: Hearth, Belfast

1997
(L) St Patrick's Church, Ballymena
Replacing & repairing tracery stonework to windows. Raking out
& repointing random stone work, sandstone buttresses & window
surrounds. Rebedding sandstone copings
Architect: Brian Campbell Structural & Civil Engineer

1997
(L) No. 7, The Square, Cushendun
Reslating mansard roof with salvaged slates, repairs to windows,
leadwork, repairs to lath & lime plaster and painting
Architect: Hearth, Belfast

1997
(L) Old Church Tower, Ballymoney
Stabilisation of disued church tower, including repointing &
brickwork repairs, provision of roof & replacement of internal
floors

UAHS ref no. 78

Sub-Contractor – Stone, Brick, Slating & Roofing, Joinery, Plasterwork

76

MAIN CONTRACTOR

M Girvan & Sons
15 The Cairn, Bush Road
Dungannon
Co. Tyrone BT71 6QB

Telephone: 018687 23183   **Fax:** 018687 27341

Contact: Maurice Girvan or Andrew Girvan

Size of Firm: 10–50 people
Works throughout Northern Ireland

Specialisation: All aspects of reconstruction

Background: In business for 30 years

Membership: Building & Civil Engineering Federation, NHBC

Examples of Work: 1993
(L) Barn, The Argory, Moy, Co. Tyrone
Refurbishment of 1820s barn to form education centre, for the
National Trust
Architect: R Robinson & Sons, Ballymoney

1995
(L) North Queen Street, Belfast
Construction of new extensions to nursing home
Architect: Barnes McCrum Partnership, Belfast

1997
(L) University Square, Belfast
Refurbishment of three listed properties in Queen's Conservation
Area
Consultant: James Clark & Partners, Belfast

1996
(L) St Molua's Parish Church, Stormont, Belfast
Repairs & replacement of circular bays
Architect: D S C Partnership, Belfast

UAHS ref no. 272

Also: Sub-Contractor – Stone, Brick, Joinery, Plasterwork, Slating & Roofing, Tiles & Tiling

MAIN CONTRACTOR

Roy Hanna & Sons
5 Colban Crescent
Lurgan BT66 8HY

Telephone: 01762 326528   **Mobile:** 0802 658698

Contact: Roy Hanna & Sons

Size of Firm: 1–10 people
Works throughout Northern Ireland

Specialisation: Joinery, stonework, external works, drainage, roads & paths, brickwork, slating & roofing

Membership: Construction Employers Federation Ltd., Building Guarantee Scheme NI Ltd.

Examples of Work: 1996
(L) Private country house, Portadown
Renovation & repairs to out-houses
Architect: Harry Porter Architects, Portadown

1996
(L) Friends Meeting House, Lurgan
Repairs & conversion
Architect: Maurice Cushnie Architects, Portadown

1993
(L) Stewart's Place, Holywood
Extensive repairs & refurbishment of four storey house
Architect: Hearth, Belfast

1997
Private country house, Berwick Hall, Moria
Renovation to house & outbuildings
Architect: Consarc Conservation, Belfast

UAHS ref no. 79

Also: Sub-Contractor – Stone, Brick, Slating & Roofing, Joinery

78

MAIN CONTRACTOR

Francis Haughey Building & Civil Engineering Contractor
21–23 St Patrick's Street
Keady
Co. Armagh BT60 3TQ

Telephone: 01861 531391   **Fax:** 01861 538739

Contact: Francis Haughey

Size of Firm: 10–50 people
Works throughout Northern Ireland

Specialisation: Stone masonry, bricklaying, & chimney repair
Roofing & slating
Purpose made joinery, plasterwork & tiling
Gates, railings & cobble paving
DPCs & waterproofing

Background: Stone masons and builders for many generations

Membership: NHBC, Federation of Building & Civil Engineering Contractors

Examples of Work: 1991
(L) Memorial, Armagh
Renovations to memorial & garden inc. granite steps &
surrounds, wrought iron railings, cobbled paths & seating
Architect: Ian Donaldson Architects, Armagh

1992
(L) Private houses, Castle Street & environs, Armagh
Major scheme of restoration for Hearth Housing Association
Awarded Europa Nostra Medal 1996

1993
(L) Heritage centre, Palace Demesne, Armagh
Conversion of traditional stone out-buildings to heritage centre
Architect: Ian Donaldson Architects, Armagh

1995/96
(L) Sharp's House, Gosford Demesne, Markethill
Major scheme of renovation & repair of 17th century dwelling
Architect: Hearth, Belfast

UAHS ref no. 127

Also: Sub-Contractor – Stone, Brick, Slating & Roofing, Joinery, Plasterwork,
Ironmongery & Metalwork, Tiles & Tiling, Remedial Works
Services & Utilities – Electrician, Plumber

MAIN CONTRACTOR

KARL Construction Limited
92 Old Ballyrobin Road
Antrim
Co. Antrim

Telephone: 01849 425600   **Fax:** 01849 428178

Contact: Gayle Davidson

Size of Firm: 350+ people
Works throughout Ireland, Scotland & England

Specialisation: KARL offers particular expertise in building contracting, structural and civil engineering, pre-stressed concrete component design and manufacture, and the maintenance and erection of pre-cast concrete structures

Background: KARL's experience has enabled it to work in a variety of capacities in addition to that of main contractor. These include turnkey projects, design and build projects, joint ventures, partnerships and consortia ventures including involvement with governments and private finance initiatives clients.

Membership: Construction Quality Assurance: (ISO 9002) Accreditation, N.I. Chamber of Commerce, Construction Employers Federation, British Institute of Facilities Management, CBI, IoD

Examples of Work: 1998
(L) Parliament Buildings, Stormont, Belfast
Complete restoration of existing parliamentary buildings
Architect: David Sayer, DoE Construction Service

1997
(L) Old Police Station, Cultra
Reconstruction of the old RUC station at the Ulster Folk and Transport Museum

1996
Fermanagh House, Belfast
Restoration of exterior and interior
Architect: David Sayer, DOE Construction Service

ongoing
Several large new-build contracts

UAHS ref no. 556

MAIN CONTRACTOR

Noel Killen Building Contractor
233A Newcastle Road
Seaforde
Co. Down BT30 9EP

Telephone: 01396 811689

Contact: Noel Killen

Size of Firm: 1–10 people
Works within a 30 miles radius of Seaforde

Specialisation: Restoration of vernacular & industrial buildings using traditional methods & materials
Roofing work inc. random & peg-hung slates; purpose made joinery & carpentry; plasterwork; structural timber repairs using cut & hand crafted reclaimed timber; & repairs & re-pointing to stonework & brick using lime mortar

Background: Over 25 years in the building trade, trained as a joiner with Co. Down building company, 20 years self-employed with own business

Membership: Guild of Master Craftsmen

Examples of Work: 1997
Farmbuildings, Island Taggart, Strangford Lough
(L) Repairs to traditional farm buildings for the National Trust
Architect: Marcus Patton

1997
(L) 13 English Street, Downpatrick
Extensive repairs to listed building including repointing with lime putty and reroofing
Architect: Raymond Press, Downpatrick

1998
Old Mill, Balleevey, Banbridge
Extensive repairs and conversion to private dwelling
Architect: Des Ewing

1998
(L) Church Road, Crossgar
Conversion of mill to private dwelling
Architect: Rachel Bevan, Downpatrick

UAHS ref no. 132

Also: Sub-Contractor – Stone, Brick, Slating & Roofing, Joinery

MAIN CONTRACTOR

Joseph McClune & Sons
205 Main Street
Dundrum
Co. Down BT33 0LY

Telephone: 013967 51223   **Fax:** 013967 51556

Contact: David McClune

Size of Firm: 10–50 people
Works throughout Northern Ireland

Specialisation: Joinery
Roofing
Brickwork & Stonework
Plastering & Pointing
Leadwork

Background: Firm established in 1917, specialising in traditional building

Membership: Construction Employers Federation

Examples of Work: 1994
Killyleagh Castle, Co. Down
(L) Re-roofing, re-pointing, replacement & repairs to leadwork,
& provision of new windows to important historic building

1995
(L) Private house, Saintfield
Major scheme of refurbishment & extension to listed gate lodge
Architect: Dawson Stelfox, Belfast

1996
(L) St Columba's Church, Kings Road, Belfast
New choir vestry
Architect: A & E Wright, Belfast

1998
(L) Almshouses, Seaforde
Window repairs and replacements
Architect: Hearth

UAHS ref no. 121

*Also: Sub-Contractor – Stone & Brick, Slating & Roofing, Leadwork,
Joinery & Cabinetmaking*

MAIN CONTRACTOR

McNally Contractors
Randalstown Limited
105 Magheralane Road
Randalstown
Co. Antrim

Telephone: 01849 472096   **Fax:** 01849 473623

Contact: Jim McNally

Size of Firm: 10–50 people
Works in Belfast, county Antrim and north Down

Specialisation: General building and restoration work
Plasterwork
Joinery
External work including fencing, paving and excavation

Background: The company has over 10 years experience in all aspects of
building work

Membership: Construction Employers Federation, National House Builders
Building Guarantee Scheme

Examples of Work: 1998
(L) Alexandra Park Gate Lodge, Belfast
complete refurbishment of vandalised property, including external
works, repairs to stonework & all internal works
Architect: Hearth, Belfast

1990's
(L) Glens of Antrim
Complete refurbishment and external works to vacant rural
cottages
Architect: Marcus Patton for Northern Ireland Tourist Board

1997
(L) Clifton Street, Belfast
Alterations and refurbishment of listed building for the Indian
Community
Architect: Dennis Piggott

UAHS ref no. 519

See also: Plasterwork, joinery

MAIN CONTRACTOR

Felix O'Hare & Co. Ltd.
88 Chancellors Road
Newry
Co. Down BT35 8LS

Telephone: 01693 61134 **Fax:** 01693 61397

Contact: John Parr

Size of Firm: 100+ people
Works throughout Northern Ireland

Specialisation: Main contractors involved in all aspects of building work
Joinery workshop with operatives experienced in specialist work
Stonework
Slating & roofing

Background: In business for 100 years

Membership: Construction Employers Federation, CBI,
Guild of Master Craftsmen

Examples of Work: 1993
(L) St Patrick's Trian Visitors Centre, Armagh
Refurbishment of old buildings & construction of interpretative
centre including offices & conservatory
Architect: Ian Donaldson Architects, Armagh

1991
(L) Newry Cathedral
Internal alterations
Architect: McLean & Forte, Belfast

1990
(L) Church, Warrenpoint
Construction of extension & alterations
Architect: McLean & Forte, Belfast

1994
St Brigids Parish Church, Belfast
Architect: Kennedy Fitzgerald & Associates, Belfast

UAHS ref no. 149

Also: Sub-Contractor – all trades

84

MAIN CONTRACTOR

Stafford & Co.
6 Northland Terrace
Dungannon
Co. Tyrone BT71 6BB

Telephone: 01868 722839   **Fax:** 01868 724922

Contact: Rowley Stafford

Size of Firm: 1–10 people
Works in Belfast & counties Tyrone & Armagh

Specialisation: General restoration work, especially church work
Building maintenance on all types of property
Joinery workshop with experienced staff
All other trades employed

Background: Company has been in business for 30 years under personal
supervision of Rowley Stafford

Membership: CITB, Construction Employers Federation and Building
Guarantee Scheme Ltd.

Examples of Work: 1998
(L) Richhill Parish Church, Richhill
Re-roofing to slated roofs, replacement leadwork and roof
timbers
Architect: Leighton Johnston Associates, Belfast

1997
Richhill Parish Church, Richhill
Re-roofing to Tower and Specialist Leadwork
Architect: Leighton Johnston Associates, Belfast

1996
(L) St Anne's Church, Dungannon
Replacement leadwork, slating & specialist joinery
Architect: Leighton Johnston Associates, Belfast

1994
Moygashel, Dungannon
New church hall
Architect: Leighton Johnston Associates, Belfast

UAHS ref no. 427

Also: Sub-Contractor – all trades

MAIN CONTRACTOR

Thorndene Developments Ltd.
108a Shore Road
Nunsquarter
Kircubbin
Co. Down BT22 2RP

Telephone: 012477 38379   **Fax:** 012477 38099

Contact: Raymond J Gilmore

Size of Firm: 10–50 people
Works throughout Northern Ireland

Specialisation: Restoration of listed buildings, historic houses and churches

Background: 30 years' experience in all aspects of building, including public & private housing, restoration of churches & listed buildings inc. work for the National Trust during past 10 years

Membership: Builders Federation, Construction Employers Federation Ltd.

Examples of Work: 1993
(L) Castle Ward, Strangford
Major scheme of restoration inc. complete re-roofing, new leadwork, stonework repairs, & internal repairs
Architect: Maurice Cushnie Architects, Portadown

(L) Mount Stewart, Co. Down
Extensive refurbishment inc. re-roofing, new leadwork, stonework repairs & replacement, & internal works
Architect: R Robinson & Sons, Ballymoney

1994
(L) Bank, Newtownards
Complete new roof, leadwork, electrical work & refurbishment to interior
Architect: Brian Emerson Associates, Hillsborough

1998
(L) Castle Ward, Strangford
Internal restructuring & refurbishment of apartments
Architect: H Rolston, Belfast

UAHS ref no. 131

Also: Sub-Contractor – all trades

1 MASONRY – STONE AND BRICK

Dressed, or finely cut, stonework is comparatively rare in Ireland, it was mainly used on grand houses, churches and public buildings. Many buildings are in rubble stone, often limewashed or rendered; however for the last hundred years brick has been the predominant material.

Unfortunately through time some of the skills and appreciation of the demands in working with stone have been lost. In the recent past it was difficult to get the right advice, the right materials and the craftsmen to work sympathetically on stone. Now the climate has changed, there is a revival of interest and it is possible now to have good work carried out – there are no longer any excuses for botched repairs and alterations.

Stone buildings weather, often attractively, but pollutants can disfigure and decay. There is a long and inglorious history of attempts to slow down and stop this weathering process; many techniques have caused more damage than if the building was left alone.

Stone walls need to breathe and need to remain flexible. Lime should be the basis for mortars, grouts, washes and renders. Some superior work made use of hydraulic lime which has a degree of natural 'set' akin to cement, but most construction work made use of pure, non-hydraulic lime in the form of lime putty mixed with aggregate. This material can only harden when in contact with air and in some circumstances may take many years to set completely. The great advantage, however, is that unlike cement and the stronger hydraulic limes, pure lime putty is porous, thereby allowing moisture entering the fabric of the building to evaporate and escape. It is also flexible so accommodating minor structural movement without cracking. Lime putty is now readily available from suppliers in Northern Ireland and the Republic of Ireland.

Cement render is not a suitable material for use on a historic building and is not a cure for damp problems. A thick porous lime plaster coating will give the best weatherproofing and durability results on solid masonry walls.

Cleaning, if necessary at all, is an expert's job, a complex process that requires a sensitive touch and deep understanding. High pressure grit blasting and indiscriminate use of powerful chemicals have caused enormous damage and must be avoided. Newer, gentler methods have been developed and are already in use. Above all, a full survey of the building needs to be carried out before any decisions are made, samples taken and tests done to determine appropriate repair, replacement and cleaning methods. Then a very detailed specification should be drawn up to ensure that the work is carried out correctly; good site supervision is essential.

Stone walls are usually thick, 400–600mm is common, and inherently stable though the enlargement of openings or breaking out new ones can be hazardous and should only be carried out with professional advice. Walls do move, bend, twist and lean and in modest buildings may have little or no foundations. Such problems do not usually require panic measures but an acceptance that old structures will not necessarily be square, plumb or true. Lime mortars and renders remain flexible and can accommodate such movements. Attempts to straighten walls will both remove the character and prove enormously expensive. External French drains, damp proof membranes in floors and electro-osmotic damp proof courses can alleviate damp penetration and, in most cases, original walls can be retained.

Whilst building or repairing rubble stone walls is within the capability of good bricklayers and local masons, provided they observe and follow the pattern of the original and do not invent their own vertical crazy paving, ashlar and dressed stone is a specialist task. There are firms of experienced stone masons working in Northern Ireland who can repair and replicate fine stonework, and although much of the new stone currently used in decorative work is imported, many types of building stone are available from quarries in the British Isles. Statuary and sculpture require the most skilled of all conservators.

Brick buildings abound in the urban areas of Ireland although there are few of the classic Georgian terraces left in Belfast, or indeed Ulster, to match those of Dublin. Bricks were made in local brickyards and often the names, such as Hampton, Laganvale or Annadale, were stamped into the clay. Most local bricks are bright red, a product of the local clays, but a burnt purply red, which has weathered to a very deep shade, is common. They are almost impossible to reproduce in new brick but can be obtained on the salvaged brick market. Many old bricks were to an 'imperial' size, deeper than the modern metric brick and of a different, more solid character when built. Some brick companies still manufacture a limited range in 'imperial' sizes. Seventeenth and eighteenth century bricks were often quite irregular and did not follow standard sizes at all.

Traditional brick walls were solid, 9" or greater, with a variety of bonds which give both strength and character. Most modern walls are of cavity construction which inevitably means a simple stretcher bond. Extensions to old buildings should respect the original bond types, either by using 'snapped' headers or a solid wall construction with the damp kept at bay by the 'breathability' of the wall and insulation taken care of on the inner face.

Old bricks are invariably uneven. Lime mortar, as with stone, allows for flexibility and ensures that the shrinkage cracks, associated with modern hard cements, will not occur.

The classic yellow stock bricks, often used in chimneys and quoins, and the blue engineering bricks, found in plinths, were mostly imported from areas with those colours of clays and are usually very dense and of high quality. Salvaged bricks should again be the first choice but good reproductions can be obtained.

The pointing of stone and brickwork is critical to its character. A lime based mortar should be used, not hard cement, for the general principle of pointing is that the joints should be weaker than the brick or stone. Raised or strap pointing is nearly always wrong. Instead joints should be raked back to a depth of at least twice the height of the joint and the new mortar brought forward until nearly flush with the edges of the stone or brick, not covering them or smeared over the surface, and struck slightly (splayed from the top down) to throw the water off. Any mortar used in historic work should be in the range 1:3 lime putty to sand up to 1:2:9 cement to lime putty to sand. The joints can then be rubbed down with a hessian bag or a soft bristle brush when nearly dry to expose the aggregate which should be chosen to match the original in colour and texture. In rubble stone work with wide joints 'snecking', small stones set within the mortar, is often found.

In ashlar work, with very tight joints, special techniques and grouts are required to pack the mortar into the joints and keep the surface clean.

Rubble stonework was rarely built to be seen and the current fashion for stripping off the render can lead to rainwater penetration as well as aesthetically being unattractive.

Research into the most appropriate ways of using lime as a material for repairing historic buildings and monuments is ongoing. Please contact the UAHS for additional information on this subject.

STONEWORK REPAIRS

This is a complex subject which requires expert guidance. The choice of techniques available is outlined below in a simplified form.

The first step in any repair scheme is to evaluate the existing state of the stonework and the degree of intervention and repair necessary. This evaluation has implications for the types of repair techniques to be undertaken and their application as exhibited by different stones or elements of the building. When various methods of repair are matched to particular stone problems, sometimes in one building or even a single façade, this is referred to as a 'palette of techniques'. The overriding principle is to retain as much as possible of the original stone.

Repair Techniques

a) Complete stone replacement:

This is an extreme measure, rarely necessary and very expensive, involving the complete rebuilding of a façade or building. It is often difficult to obtain original or compatible stone and this solution should only be used when there is complete failure of the stone or metal fixings.

b) Replacement of individual stones:

Weathering of stone is endlessly variable and individual stones may fail for many reasons – surface spalling, fixing failure, structural movement etc. Geological matching is critical to ensure compatibility of future weathering. Stones can be replaced either to full depth or, more commonly, to 75–100mm thickness, depending on the amount of decay of the original stone. Fixings may be necessary and should be of stainless steel to avoid corrosion.

c) Indenting:

Where only a small section of an original stone is damaged – e.g. by rusting around a railing fixing – it is more appropriate to replace only a small section of stone. The new stone needs to be geologically matched, as noted above, to a similar 75–100mm depth, and should be tightly butted to the original, without expressing the joint, and fixed as necessary. In finer work much smaller indents are possible, often held in place with epoxy grouts.

d) Render repairs:

Large scale render or 'plastic' repairs are now largely discredited though this is a useful technique for small scale repairs to complicated carvings or sculpture. The renders must be of a 'soft' lime based mix to avoid accelerated weathering of surrounding stone. Stainless steel wire cages can be used to build up profiles. This is a technique for expert conservators, not a cheap alternative to correct stone repairs.

e) Consolidants:

Chemical consolidants can delay weathering of stone and help delay or avoid replacement. However, the associated chemistry and geology is complex and specialist scientific and laboratory assistance is required with full testing before application.

f) Redressing:

When surface failure has occurred a technique sometimes considered is the redressing of the stonework to its original profile. This is a skilled stonemasons' task. It is possible to reface chemically consolidated stonework as discussed under item (e), particularly rock faced walling that shows facial deterioration. Generally only 15–25mm of the decayed stone is removed to allow realignment to the original profile. This technique is used for decayed stone deeply embedded within a wall which itself has minimal decay yet is disfigured. Door cases and window cills are particular examples on which this technique can be used.

See also   *Section 3 Leadwork (for flashings etc.) – p. 112*
                 Section 4 Metalwork (for metal cramps and fixings) – p. 118
                 Section 6 Plasterwork (for external renders) – p. 137
                 Section 11 Remedial Works (for DPCs and other treatments) – p. 167

                 Appendix 1: Further reading – p. 199

Sub-Contractor – STONE

Architectural Stonemasonry Partnership
25 Mount Alverno
Dermott Hill Park
Springfield Road
Belfast BT12 7GL

Telephone: 01232 312659   **Fax:** 01960 373605

Contact: Paul Clarke

Size of Firm: 1–10 people
Works throughout Northern Ireland

Specialisation: Stone restoration, stone walling, dressing of stone for building

Background: Served apprenticeship at Carrickfergus Castle with the Historic Monuments and Buildings Branch

Examples of Work: 1998
(L) North Street Presbyterian Church, Carrickfergus
Restoration of pilasters, pediment, strings, quoins and doorway (sandstone Ballyalton). Cleaning and pointing

1998
(L) Drumbeg, Lisburn
Restoration of gate lodge pillars and boundary walling. Carving of new capitals
Architect: Alister Gilcrest, Knox & Markwell, Bangor

Carrickfergus
Stone pillars & walling
Architect: Stanley O'Neil, Knox & Markwell, Bangor

1994
(L) Maghramourne House Hotel Entrance
Building of circular pillars & coursed random rubble walling

UAHS ref no. 562

Also: Sub-Contractor – Stonecarving and Restoration

Sub-Contractor – STONE

Architectural Stonemasonry Partnership
11 Victoria Avenue
Whitehead
Carrickfergus
Co. Antrim BT38 9AF

Telephone: 01960 372818   **Fax:** 01960 373605

Contact: Hector Nelson

Size of Firm: 1–10 people
Works throughout Northern Ireland

Specialisation: Stone carving, stone restoration, stone building & dressing of stone for building
Skilled in all aspects of masonry
Supervisory & Planning works if required

Background: Served apprenticeship with Historic Monuments & Building Branch
Worked on the Forest Place Complex, Perth, N. Australia, as a stonemason

Membership: City & Guilds of London Craft Certificate in Masonry

Examples of Work: 1998
(L) Old Mill, Dunadry, Co. Antrim
The restoration of the Old Mill using coursed basalt stone to match existing building
Architect: Glen Philpott

1998
(L) Church of Ireland, Carnmoney, Newtownabbey
Restoration, carving, building & pointing of church tower & main body
Architect: Mr Billy Hunter, R Robinson & Sons

1998
(L) Loughgall, Co. Armagh, Dept. of Agriculture
Restoration & carving of Griffins placed on top of main entrance pillars
Architect: John Mansfield

1996
(L) Church of Ireland, Co. L'Derry
Restoration and repointing of church & tower
Architect: Mr Billy Hunter, R Robinson & Sons

UAHS ref no. 524

Also: Sub-Contractor – Stonecarvings, Restoration

Sub-Contractor – STONE

Con-Tech Associates (Ireland) Ltd.
Unit 3, Doagh Mill
Mill Road
Doagh
Co. Antrim BT39 0PQ

Telephone: 01960 341116   **Fax:** 01960 341118

Contact: Paul Thompson – Contracts Manager

Size of Firm: 1–10 people
Works throughout Northern Ireland

Specialisation: The cleaning and restoration of natural stone and brick
Conservation and restoration of monumental bronze

Examples of Work: 1998
(L) Hillhall Presbyterian Church, Lisburn
Cleaning and restoration of natural stone
Architect: WDR & RT Taggart, Belfast

1998
(L) McCausland Building, Victoria Street, Belfast
Cleaning and restoration of natural stone & brickwork
Architect: Edmondson Cosgrove & Robinson, Dublin

1997
Craigavon Civic Centre
Removal, restoration and refixing of two bronze Coats of Arms
Architect: Wheelan & Co., Lurgan

1996
(L) Tesco Metro, Royal Avenue, Belfast
Paint removal, repairs, repainting etc., of natural stone
Consultant: Lithian Ltd., Newtownards

UAHS ref no. 112

Also: Sub-Contractor – Brick, Monumental Bronze, Painterwork
Main contractor – Stone

Sub-Contractor – STONE

Adrian Curran Stone Mason Gothic Craft
3B Derryola Island Lane
Gawleys Gate
Aghalee
Co. Armagh BT67 0DN

Telephone: 01846 652607 / 01762 325498

Contact: Adrian Curran

Size of Firm: 1–10 people
Works throughout Northern Ireland

Specialisation: Skilled in all aspects of masonry, carving & stonework restoration
Experienced in supervising masonry work
Stone masonry surveying & detailing available

Background: 17 years' experience with Environment and Heritage Service –
Historic Monuments
Competition winner for design & execution of monument in
public park, Portadown
City & Guilds of London Advanced Masonry Certificate
ONC & HNC in Building Studies

Examples of Work: (L) City Hall, Belfast
Repairs to statue of Queen Victoria
Architect: Consarc Design Group Ltd., Belfast

1996
(L) Custom House, Belfast
Foreman mason on project, inc. completion of major repairs to
statues
Architect: Consarc Design Group Ltd., Belfast

(M) Newtownards Priory & Town Hall
Repairs & carving work to doorway, for Environment and
Heritage Service – Historic Monuments

1997
(L) Killyleagh Castle, Killyleagh
Supervised restoration of walls, repointing using lime mortar,
recarving balustrade walling
Contractor: W Dowling

UAHS ref no. 448

94

Sub-Contractor – STONE

The Global Stone Company Limited
Musgrave Park Industrial Estate
Belfast BT9 9ET

Telephone: 01232 381220   **Fax:** 01232 381240

Contact: Sandra Bleakley & Paul McAlister

Size of Firm: 10–50 people
Works throughout Northern Ireland

Specialisation: Specialists in all aspects of natural stone:
Consultation, design, sourcing, supply, fixing, carving,
conservation, restoration, cleaning, protection

Background: Staff include a geologist and architect, quantity surveyor and
specialist with expertise in new technologies for cleaning stone &
the application of protective coatings. Experienced stone masons.
Staff have attended SPAB courses and seminars at the Building
Research Establishment

Membership: UAHS, Building Limes Forum, Society for the Protection of
Ancient Buildings, Construction Employers Federation,
Construction Industry Training Board, National Anti Graffiti
Association

Examples of Work: 1998
(L) Alexandra Park Gate Lodge, Belfast
Source, supply and repair of replacement stone
Architect: Marcus Patton, Hearth

1998
St Vincent de Paul Church, Ligoniel, Belfast
Supply and repair of replacement sandstone, restoration mortar,
repointing. Exterior cleaning and carving
Architect: J. J. Brennan & Co.

1997
J. Sainsbury, Forestside, Belfast
Cleaning of building exterior and application of sacrificial coating
Architect: Ostick and Williams

1997
Indian Community Centre, Clifton Street, Belfast
Cleaning of sandstone and limestone building
Architect: Dennis Piggott

UAHS ref no. 467

*See also: Quantity surveyor, architectural stone consultant, fireplaces, stone
cleaning & protective coatings*

Sub-Contractor – STONE

Kevin Lappin Stone Mason
Coney Island
Ardglass
Co. Down BT30

Telephone: 01396 841358

Contact: Kevin Lappin

Size of Firm: 1–10 people
Works throughout Northern Ireland

Specialisation: Random rubble walling
Dry stone walling
Building of dressed stone, ashlar & sandstone
Pointing work
Bricklaying

Background: Fully qualified bricklayer
Long family tradition of stone building

Examples of Work: 1994
Private house, Killough, Co. Down
Taking down & complete reconstruction of former stone built
coach house, to form new house – within the Killough
Conservation Area
Architect: George Sampson, Killough

1996
The Narrows Guest House, Portaferry
Stone & brickwork in and around courtyard – in Portaferry
Conservation Area
Architect: Rachel Bevan, Downpatrick

1995
(L) Rowallane House, Saintfield
Taking down & re-building entrance pillars, for the National Trust
Main Contractor: Castle Contracts, Dundrum

1997–98
(L) Aughnacloy Old Mill
Restoration & rebuild
Contractor: Woodvale Construction, Omagh

UAHS ref no. 455

Also: Sub-Contractor – Brick

Sub-Contractor – STONE

Lithan Ltd.
5B Ards Business Centre
Newtownards
Co. Down BT23 4YH

Telephone: 01247 819787 ext. 221   **Fax:** 01247 820625

Contact: John Kelly

Size of Firm: 1–10 people
Works throughout Ireland

Specialisation: Conservation & restoration of stone objects
Conservation & restoration of monumental bronze

Background: Formerly Senior Conservator, Ulster Museum with responsibility
for ceramics, glass & stone

Membership: IPCRA, ICOMOS, ICHAW, UKIC, MGC Conservation Register

Examples of Work: (L) Private building, Belfast
Treatment of marble statuary
Architect: R McKinstry, Lisburn

Public Records Office, Belfast
Treatment of stone & plaster statuary

(L) Cashel Abbey / Ardfert Abbey
Conservation & restoration of carved detail, for the Office of
Public Works

Portadown
Conservation & restoration of bronze statuary for private client

UAHS ref no. 338

*Also: Consultant – Analysis & Specification of Stone & Related Materials – p. 58
Sub-Contractor – Monumental Bronze*

Sub-Contractor – STONE

Mourne Stone Craft
63 Longstone Road
Moneydarragh
Annalong
Co. Down BT34 4UY

Telephone: 016937 68222   **Fax:** 016937 67048

Contact: John McKibbin

Size of Firm: 10–50 people
Works throughout Northern Ireland

Specialisation: Experts in natural stone
Building, cladding and cleaning

Background: 50 years experience

Examples of Work: 1994
(L) St Peter's Cathedral, Belfast
Walls, pillars and steps
Architect: McKenna Design

1996
(L) City Hall, Belfast
Pillars, base stones for railings, steps and ramp
Architect: Consarc Design Group, Belfast

1996
(L) Custom House, Belfast
Granite steps, balusters, coping and window arches
Architect: Consarc Design Group, Belfast

1998
Seatown Castle, Dundalk, Co. Louth
Architect: Brendan G Cashel, Dundalk

UAHS ref no. 171

Sub-Contractor – STONE

J & J Mowbray & Co.
5 Kenbella Parade
Belfast BT15 5DX
Telephone: 01232 781447   **Fax:** 01232 781449

Contact: James Mowbray

Size of Firm: 10–50 people
Works throughout Northern Ireland

Specialisation: Restoration & replacement of stone
Cleaning of stone & bronze

Background: Staff training in association with the Construction Industry
Training Board

Membership: Construction Employers Federation

Examples of Work: 1993
(L) City Hall, Belfast
Repairs, cleaning & re-bronzing of statuary
Architect: Consarc Design Group Ltd., Belfast

1993
(L) Church, Donegall Street, Belfast
Cleaning & replacement of stone, consolidation of stonework &
re-pointing
Architect: McLean & Forte, Belfast

1994
(L) Cathedral, Armagh
Cleaning, replacement of stone, & re-pointing

1994
Private building, Londonderry
Cleaning & replacement of stone, consolidation of stonework &
re-pointing, & works to decorative carvings
Consulting Engineer: J C Warnock, Londonderry

UAHS ref no. 336

Also: Sub-Contractor – Monumental Bronze

Sub-Contractor – STONE

	Thomas Rooney & Sons Stonemasons
	Heather Heights, 147 Head Road
	Ballymartin, Kilkeel
	Co. Down BT34 4PX
Telephone:	013967 68365

Contact: Thomas Rooney

Size of Firm: 1–10 people
Works throughout Northern Ireland

Specialisation: Construction of hand worked stone walls, pillars, fireplaces, chimneys & garden beds

Background: 30 years' experience of building in stone

Examples of Work: 1997
Private dwelling, Carlingford
Stone construction

1996
Ulster Folk & Transport Museum, Cultra
Reconstruction of Mourne cottage & byre

1994
Purdysburn, Banbridge & Portadown
Construction of stone walls & pillars

1992
Golf club, Belfast
Restoration & reconstruction of stone wall in grounds

1992
Private house, Annalong, Co. Down
Construction of stone wall

UAHS ref no. 168

Sub-Contractor – STONE

Stonecarve
89A Slievegallion Drive
Belfast BT11 8JP

Telephone: 01232 613114 / 624500

Contact: Eamon McCann

Size of Firm: 1–10 people
Works throughout Northern Ireland

Specialisation: Stonecarver
Architectural work eg. capitals & quoins, figure and foliage carving, lettering, coats of arms
Cleaning & repairs to stone mouldings & detailing

Background: BA (Hons) Fine Art
City and Guilds of London Advanced Masonry Certificate
Carving & sculptural work as sub-contractor for a number of firms in Northern Ireland

Examples of Work: 1991
(L) Thompson Memorial, Ormeau Avenue, Belfast
Carved new stone figure heads to match original, decayed heads
Architect: Hearth, Belfast

1994
Private apartments, Donaghadee
Built new, three storey, basalt tower house in grounds of listed building, for use as apartments

1996
(L) Custom House, Belfast
Major works to stone capitals inc. cutting out damaged stone, carving replacements & re-fixing
Architect: Consarc Design Group Ltd.

1996
(L) Dunbreen Bridge
Restoration of original stone plaque on bridge, work carried out in workshop

UAHS ref no. 328

Sub-Contractor – STONE

Stone Restoration Services
6 Marchioness Green
Belfast BT12 4LA

Telephone: 01232 2447735   **Mobile:** 0411 085470

Contact: Michael Barrett

Size of Firm: 1–10 people
Works throughout Northern Ireland

Specialisation: Specialist in architectural and ecclesiastical stone masonry for example, stone carving, stone restoration, pointing, construction of tracery windows

Background: City and Guilds of London Masonry Certificate
All employees are qualified craftsmen

Examples of Work: 1998
(L) Alexandra Park Gate Lodge
Recarving and replacement of defective rock face and dressed stonework
Architect: Marcus Patton, Hearth

1997
(L) St Patrick's Church, Ballymena
Construction of tracery window
Architect: Brian Campbell

1996
(L) Temple of the Winds, Mount Stewart
Dismantling and reconstruction of cornice and all restoration and stone replacement
Architect: A & E Wright

1994
(L)
Somerset Studios, Belfast
Complete pointing using cleanpoint brick pointing system and pressure washing
Architect: Boyd Partners

UAHS ref no. 521

Sub-Contractor – STONE

Castle Contracts – p. 73
T Chambers & Sons (Enniskillen) Ltd. – p. 74
Con-Tech Associates (Ireland) Ltd. – p. 93
William Dowling Ltd. – p. 75
J S Dunlop – p. 76
M Girvan – p. 77
Roy Hanna & Sons – p. 78
Francis Haughey – p. 79
Noel Killen – p. 81
Lithan Ltd. – p. 97
Joseph McClune & Sons – p. 82
Dan McPolin at Narrow Water Lime Service – p. 52
Felix O'Hare – p. 84
O'Neill Bros. (Building Contractors) Ltd. – p. 130
Stafford & Co. – p. 85
Thorndene Developments – p. 86

Sub-Contractor – BRICK

Jose Alves-Areias – p. 70
Castle Contracts – p. 73
Castle Glen – p. 153
T Chambers & Sons (Enniskillen) Ltd. – p. 74
Con-Tech Associates (Ireland) Ltd. – p. 93
William Dowling Ltd. – p. 75
J S Dunlop – p. 76
M Girvan & Sons – p. 77
Roy Hanna & Sons – p. 78
Francis Haughey – p. 79
Noel Killen – p. 81
Kevin Lappin (Stone Mason) – p. 96
Joseph McClune & Sons – p. 82
Dan McPolin at Narrow Water Lime Service – p. 52
Felix O'Hare – p. 84
O'Neill Bros. (Building Contractors) Ltd. – p. 130
Stafford & Co. – p. 85
Thorndene Developments – p. 86

Sub-Contractor – MONUMENTAL BRONZE

Con-Tech Associates (Ireland) Ltd. – p. 93
Lithan Ltd. – p. 58, 97
J & J Mowbray & Co. – p. 99

2 ROOFING – SLATING, TILING AND THATCH

Thatch is the traditional roofing material of Ireland and was almost universal in modest houses until the mid nineteenth century. Locally available split stone or slate was used but it was not until the widespread availability of cheap Welsh slate that the major changes occurred. Slate required little maintenance, was easily worked, attractive, and remained the main roofing material until very recent times. Widespread use of clay and concrete tiles has surpassed the use of slate but it remains the best material for repairs and extensions to old buildings.

Thatch has declined alarmingly – there are now fewer than 200 inhabited thatched buildings in Northern Ireland. Concern is so great for their survival outside museums that the Environment and Heritage Service are offering 75% grants towards thatching and maintenance. Old problems of damp and mould are easily solved today and while regular maintenance is required the benefits of beauty and character plus the grant available can swing the financial balance. There has been a great revival of interest in thatching in Britain and this is spreading to Northern Ireland. Thatchers are now more easily found and there is no doubt that the craft will develop with the revival of interest in thatching.

Natural slate is also enjoying a revival and with the high cost of new slate a market led demand for salvaged slate has emerged. When re-roofing is necessary careful choice is required to avoid a patchwork quilt of blues and greys as there are considerable differences in colour. It is wise to avoid mixing slates from different sources so the original ones should be kept together and used on the most prominent elevations. Delaminated slates or ones with splits or overlarge nail holes should be discarded. Variations in detail in the roofscape such as rows of particularly large slates at the eaves, called queens, diminishing courses, that is slates getting gradually smaller towards the ridge, and the ridge materials (stone, clay or lead) are of immense importance to the character of the building and should be retained. It is vital to check roofs regularly for slipped or missing slates and to repair promptly.

Westmoreland or Norwegian green slates were popular in Ireland in the inter-war years and it is still possible to get new slates to match. Clay tiles are a very old roofing material rarely found in Northern Ireland until modern times when the 'Rosemary' small plain tile became popular. Cedar shingles enjoyed a brief boom in the 1950s but in general have not fared well in the damp climate.

In general natural slate roofs should have a minimum of 35° pitch, rising to 45° or greater for small slates. Where it is not possible to lay natural slate, a different material such as lead should be used.

Finally, painted corrugated metal sheeting is a traditional roof in the country, mainly over barns and out-buildings, but often over the top of thatch on houses. Black, green or red lead are the common colours and their use should be considered on all rural building groups.

See also   *Section 3 Leadwork (for flashings) p. 112*
           Section 11 Remedial works (for chimneys) p. 167

           Appendix 1: Further reading p. 199

Sub-Contractor – SLATING & ROOFING

McArdle Brothers
4 Convent Close
Armagh BT60 4BH

Telephone: 01861 523242 / 524097   **Fax:** 01861 523242

Contact: Patrick McArdle

Size of Firm: 1–10 people
Works throughout Northern Ireland

Specialisation: Repairs & re-roofing listed buildings in new & second-hand slates
Leadwork, Penrhyn approved roofing contractor

Background: Family business for 100 years

Examples of Work: 1996
(L) St Jude's Church, Ormeau Road, Belfast
Complete re-roofing, lifting off barge stones & re-leading
Architect: Alastair Coey Architects, Belfast

(L) Ballinderry Parish Church, Lisburn
Complete re-roofing, re-leading under skews, new eaves gutter &
downpipes
Architect: Leighton Johnston Associates, Belfast

1998
(L) Campbell College, Belfast
Repairs to new house & rear yard
Consultant: V B Evans & Company, Belfast

1997
(L) Fitzroy Presbyterian Church Hall
Reslating roof, renewing lead valleys
Consultant: Leighton Johnston Associates, Belfast

UAHS ref no. 118

Also: Sub-Contractor – Leadwork

Sub-Contractor – SLATING & ROOFING

	S McMahon Roofing & Restoration	
	186B Kingsway	
	Dunmurry	
	Belfast BT17 9AD	
Telephone:	01232 617777	**Fax:** 01232 617772

Contact: Stephen McMahon

Size of Firm: 1–10 people
Works throughout Northern Ireland

Specialisation: Roofing in natural slates
Repair & renewal of leadwork
Repair & renewal of rainwater goods

Background: Apprentice 1982–84, manager of own business 1984 to date

Membership: Approved contractor for Pehrhyn slate
Member NFRC

Examples of Work: 1998
Private house, Cadogan Park, Belfast
Rake out and repoint masonry including chimneys, replacement of rainwater goods

1997
Private house, Deramore Park, Belfast
Strip and reslate main roofs using new and salvaged slate. Rebuilt chimney and replaced rainwater goods

1997
Private house, Kings Road, Belfast
Strip and reslate main roof using salvaged and new slates.
Replacement of rainwater goods

1995
(L) St Peter's Church of Ireland, Antrim Road, Belfast
Repair & restoration works inc. re-slating, renewal of leadwork & cleaning

UAHS ref no. 327

Also: Sub-Contractor – Leadwork

Sub-Contractor – SLATING & ROOFING

Penrose Roofing Limited
Trailcock Lane
Trailcock Road
Eden
Carrickfergus BT38 7NU

Telephone: 01960 351650   **Fax:** 01960 367489

Contact: Gordon C Penrose or Don C Penrose

Size of Firm: 50+ people
Works throughout Northern Ireland

Specialisation: Roof slating & roof tiling
Roof consultant
Stockist of historical roofing materials

Background: 1960–65 indentured apprentice slating & tiling, gaining City &
Guilds Advanced Craft certificate
1965–66 studied building engineering at Millfield Technical
College, Belfast
1966–67 trainee manager
1967–present director of Penrose Roofing

Membership: Past President and National Treasurer, National Federation of
Roofing Contractors
Fellow of the Institute of Roofing
Member of the Worshipful Company of Tilers & Bricklayers
(London). NIHE Approved Contractor.

Examples of Work: 1995
Queen's University, Belfast
Roof stripped & re-slated using Penryn slates
Quantity Surveyor: W H Stephens & Sons, Belfast

1996
Presbyterian church, Donegall Road, Belfast
Roof stripped & re-slated re-using existing slates & new Spanish
natural slate, replacement of leadwork & re-pointing stonework

1998
Methodist church, West Street, Carrickfergus
Roof stripped & re-slated re-using existing slates & new Spanish
natural slate, replacement of leadwork & associated building works
Architect: Johnston Stirling Tweedie & Neill, Belfast

UAHS ref no. 456

Stakis Park Hotel, Templepatrick
Roofed with Penryn slates and all associated lead work
Architect: Crerar & Partners, Scotland

Sub-Contractor – THATCH

Tom the Thatcher
14 Beechdale Avenue
Commons Road
Navan
Co. Meath

Telephone: 00 353 4671222   **Mobile:** 00 353 87276 4079

Contact: Tom O'Byrne

Size of Firm: 1–10 people
Works throughout Ireland

Specialisation: Long straw thatcher using organically grown straw imported from England
Reed, flax and rye thatching
Mud wall restoration

Background: Comes from a long line of thatchers
Served time with Peter Brokett, Master Thatcher

Examples of Work: 1998
Private House, Riverstown, Co. Meath
Large extension to previously thatched roof

1995
Private House, Ardee, Co. Louth
Rebuilt wattle and daub wall, replaced roof timbers and long straw thatch

1996
Private House, Kilmessin, Co. Meath
Long straw rethatch of restored old dwelling

1997
Private House, Meigh, Co. Armagh
Removal of slates from old roof, long straw rethatch

UAHS ref no. 566

Also: Sub-Contractor – Mud wall restoration

Sub-Contractor – THATCH

Wicklow Thatching Services Ltd.
Loen Folly
Knockrobin
Wicklow
Co. Wicklow

Telephone: 00 353 404 69846   **Fax:** 00 353 404 69846
Mobile: 00 353 288 575400

Contact: Kyran O'Grady

Size of Firm: 1–10 people
Works throughout Ireland

Specialisation: Thatching in reed, to both existing and new buildings for private
& commercial clients

Background: The company has undertaken thatching contracts for the last 17
years

Examples of Work: 1988
'Stillorgan Orchard' public house, Co. Dublin
Conversion of slated building to thatch
Architect: Brady Stanley O'Connell Assoc., Dublin

1992
Clonlee, Co. Dublin
Thatching of new corporate headquarters for KEPAK
Supervising Officer: Design & Project Management, Dublin

1993
Private house, Killyman, Dungannon
Thatching of new house

1989
Private house, Annaghmore, Portadown
Thatching of new house

UAHS ref no. 191

Sub-Contractor – SLATING & ROOFING

3 LEADWORK & COPPER ROOFING

Leadwork is still often carried out by a plumber, recalling the origin of the trade. Lead is an extremely durable and flexible material but it does demand expertise. Good detailing and practice are essential to ensure excessive thermal movement does not open joints, sag flashings or stretch large flat sheets so that they split open.

Old buildings sometime have complex roof structures with hidden gutters and valleys. Leaks are sources of problems which may be out of sight, while slow leaks saturate roof timbers and may lead to dry rot.

Valleys and valley gutters should be broad, laid to good falls and easily cleaned. Overflows should be positioned in prominent locations to warn of gutter blockages; regular maintenance is essential. In important buildings moisture sensitive alarms can be installed underneath hidden valleys to warn of damp penetration. Flashings on chimneys, parapets, abutments etc. all require well detailed lead of appropriate thickness, size and design.

The Lead Sheet Association publishes details of good practice, carries out research and offers an advice service. The Lead Contractors Association publishes a directory of specialist leadworking contractors and has four members in Northern Ireland.

These publications can be obtained from:

The Lead Contractors Association and the Lead Sheet Association
St John's Road
Tunbridge Wells
Kent TN4 9XA
Tel: 01892 513737
Fax: 01892 535028

Copper roofing is the traditional material for domes and cupolas, and correct installation is a skilled trade. It is a versatile and very attractive material, and can now be supplied in prepatinated form to avoid the problems associated with unsightly weathering in the early years.

See also   *Appendix 1: Further reading – p. 199*

Sub-Contractor – LEADWORK

Carrick Lead Supplies
Unit 19U Kilroot Business Park
Larne Road
Carrickfergus BT38 7PR

Telephone: 01960 367343   **Fax:** 01960 359844

Contact: John Wilson

Size of Firm: 1–10 people
Works throughout Northern Ireland

Specialisation: Specialists in all types of leadwork – fabrication & construction
Private housing, historical & commercial work

Background: Working with lead for 30 years

Membership: Lead Contractors Association

Examples of Work: 1997
(L) Brownlow House, Lurgan
Flat lead gutters
Architect: DSC Partnerships, Lurgan

1997
(L) St Canice's Church, Eglinton, Co Londonderry
Flat lead roof to tower
Architect: R Robinson & Sons, Ballymoney

1997
(L) St Patrick's Church, Armoy
Lead gutters & associated work to spire
Architect: The Gault Kay Partnership

1998
(L) St Patrick's Church, Ballymena
Lead capping to copings
Architect: Brian C Campbell, Ballymena

UAHS ref no. 157

Sub-Contractor – LEADWORK & COPPER

Robert A Copeland & Sons Ltd
Dunshaughlin Industrial Estate
Dunshaughlin
Co. Meath

Telephone: 00 353 1 8258055　　　　**Fax:** 00 353 1 8258088

Contact: Paul Copeland

Size of Firm: 1–10 people
Works throughout Southern Ireland

Specialisation: Specialist copper, lead and zinc roofing contractors for both traditional and modern methods

Background: Approx. 100 years of experience. All craftsmen trained in house

Membership: Construction Industry Federation
Irish Guild of Master Craftsmen

Examples of Work: 1995
(L) Mullingar Cathedral
Re-roof entire cathedral with new longstrip copper
Main Contractor: Kelly Brothers, Rosemart

1997
Herbert Street, Dublin
New zinc roof at Connaught House including Mansard roof
Arthur Gibney & Partners, Eithne Walsh

1993
(L) Sweepstake Development, Ballsbridge, Dublin 4
Lead conical roofs on 7 storey apartments
Main Contractor: Cosgrave Builders, Tom Cosgrave

UAHS ref no. 478

Also: Sub-Contractor – Coppersmiths

Sub-Contractor – LEADWORK

Leadwise Contracts
12A Cultra Avenue
Holywood
Co. Down BT18 0LT

Telephone: 01232 428100   **Fax:** 01232 428100

Contact: Martin Cahalan

Size of Firm: 1–10 people
Works throughout Northern Ireland

Specialisation: Specialist lead working contractors

Membership: Lead Contractors Association

Examples of Work: 1991
(L) Private country house, Newtownstewart, Co. Tyrone
Renewal of lead gutters & capping to stonework
Architect: Alastair Coey Architects, Belfast

1993
(L) Educational building, Belfast
Parapet gutters, lead hips & ridges, capping to stonework &
flashings
Architect: G McKnight, Holywood

1994
(L) City Hall, Belfast
Flat roofs, gutter linings
Architect: Consarc Design Group Ltd., Belfast

1996
(L) The Custom House, Belfast
Complete renewal of lead hips & ridges, weatherings to cornices,
pediments, stone plinths etc.
Architect: John Neil Partnership, Belfast

UAHS ref no. 387

Sub-Contractor – COPPER ROOFING

Edgeline Contracts Ltd.
106A Pond Park Road
Lisburn
Co. Antrim BT28 3QS

Telephone: 01846 604414   **Fax:** 01846 604416

Contact: John Wills

Size of Firm: 1–10 people
Works throughout Northern Ireland

Specialisation: Copper roofing & cladding

Membership: Metal Roofing Contractors Association
National Federation of Roofing Contractors

Examples of Work: 1994
(L) Porte-cochere, City Hall, Belfast
Prepatinated copper roofing over existing Portland stone dome
Architect: Consarc Design Group Ltd., Belfast

1994
Church of Ireland, Belvoir Park, Belfast
Long strip copper roofing
Architect: Ostick & Williams, Belfast

1995
Armagh Observatory, Armagh
Re-roofing copper dome
Architect: Leighton Johnston Associates, Belfast

1998
Clocktower, St Luke's Hospital, Armagh
Copper roofing & cladding
Quantity Surveyors: Holmes & Doran, Dungannon

UAHS ref no. 421

Sub-Contractor – LEADWORK

4 IRONMONGERY AND METALWORK

Early door and window furniture originated with the local craftsmen, blacksmiths and metal workers, and so are often unique to an area. Factory made ironmongery gradually evolved until the Victorian era when a complex variety of door and window fittings were mass produced. Many of these are again available as some firms specialise in exact reproductions of the original.

Old door furniture can be restored and if the locks fail to match modern security requirements a discreetly placed deadlock can supplement them without interfering with the character. Replacement ironmongery and fittings must be chosen carefully to match the period of the building.

In most traditional buildings gutters and downpipes are of cast iron, usually with either a half round or ogee faced box section. Although long lasting, cast iron eventually rusts away at the joints and owners often find that their gutters leak and are difficult to repair. Replacement in PVC or extruded aluminium is not the answer for old buildings though some cast aluminium systems do match the details correctly and eliminate the maintenance problems of cast iron. On historic buildings there is no substitute for replacement in new cast iron which is available with all the fittings, brackets and hoppers to match the original. One common problem is when guttering in one terrace house need to be replaced for it is difficult to patch an existing gutter. Some firms specialise in glass fibre based junction pieces for those awkward areas and this can avoid the replacement of guttering that is otherwise adequate.

Stonework often has hidden metal fixings, cramps and ties and these are invariably of iron rather than the more stable bronze. Damp penetration over the years rusts these fixings and they expand which causes the stone to crack and explode. Extensive replacement with stainless steel fixings may be necessary in serious cases but good maintenance of pointing and flashings can prevent serious problems occurring.

Restoration of industrial machinery is becoming more widespread and with it the recognition of the specialist repair and maintenance skills involved. It requires a unique blend of artistry and craft to manufacture replacement parts from the most basic of materials and to reassemble long disused machinery into working order. It is important to ensure that this machinery works thereby keeping the skills alive.

Metal balustrades, balconies, gates, railings, windows, rooflights, light brackets and a host of other fittings can be repaired or reproduced. Specialist companies produce exact copies from Victorian catalogues and skilled metal workers can repair or recast broken or missing pieces.

See also   *Appendix 1: Further reading – p. 199*

Sub-Contractor – IRONMONGERY & METALWORK

Bushey Park Ironworks
The Forge
Units 22–24 Greenhills Business Park
Tallaght
Dublin 24
Ireland

Telephone: 00 353 1 4622788   **Fax:** 00 353 1 4622790
     e-mail: bushypark@indigo.ie

Contact: Edward Bisgood or Colm Bagnall

Size of Firm: 10–50 people
Works throughout Ireland and the UK

Specialisation: Blacksmiths, combining traditional blacksmithing skills with modern machinery. Work in wrought iron, mild steel, bronze, copper & brass

Background: The company employs ten fully trained blacksmiths, three with design degrees, one engineer and eight apprentices

Membership: British Artists' Blacksmiths Association

Examples of Work: 1997
(L) Madison Hotel, Belfast
Hand forged staircase, railings, furniture & light fittings
Architect: John Duffy Architects

The Burrendale Hotel, Newcastle
Hand forged railings lights, curtain poles and balconies
Architect: Ms Joan Thompson, Architect, Banbridge

on going
(L) Powerscourt Estate, Co. Wicklow
Restoration of the largest collection of French, German & English gates and railings in Ireland
Architect: Bushy Park, in house design team

1998
(L) Castletown Cox, Co. Kilkenny
Restoration of iron work, fireplaces & railings
Hand forging of gates using only traditional blacksmithing skills
Architect: Quinlan Terry, Quinlan Terry Architects, UK

UAHS ref no. 532

Sub-Contractor – IRONMONGERY & METALWORK

McGlinchey Brothers Ltd.
Ballysillan Industrial Estate
Ligoniel Road
Belfast BT14 8EY

Telephone: 01232 713594   **Fax:** 01232 716789

Contact: James McGlinchey

Size of Firm: 10–50 people
Works throughout Northern Ireland

Specialisation: Restoration & replacement of architectural metalwork
Design, fabrication & fitting of classical ironwork
Work in mild & stainless steel

Background: Over 30 years experience

Membership: Engineering Employers Federation

Examples of Work: 1987
(L) Royal Courts of Justice, Belfast
Fabrication & erection of 4 sets of wrought steel double entrance
gates with cast iron crests & railings to existing stone balustrade
wall

1991
(L) City Hall, Belfast
Refurbishment & conversion of existing sliding gates to hinged
gates, & supply & fitting of side & head panels
Consulting Engineer: Taylor & Boyd, Belfast

1989
Ormeau Park, Belfast
Design, supply & erection of new gates & pillars

ongoing
St George's Market, Belfast
Restoration of all gates & fanlight panels
Architect: Consarc

UAHS ref no. 143

Sub-Contractor – IRONMONGERY & METALWORK

Portadown Professional Locksmith
22–24 West Street
Portadown
Co. Armagh BT62 3PL

Telephone: 01762 350767   **Fax:** 01762 350767

Contact: Philip Troughton

Size of Firm: 1–10 people
Works throughout Northern Ireland

Specialisation: General locksmiths and safe engineers. Lock restoration; keys made for locks and locks made for keys, locked doors opened. MASTER KEY systems

Background: Master Locksmiths

Membership: Company Member of Master Locksmiths Association, Irish Locksmiths Association

Examples of Work: (L) Robinson Library, Armagh
Locks restored and keys made

(L) Armagh Courthouse
Master Key System to suit existing doors and style after bomb damage

The Science Museum, London
Supply of cam-locks and special keys

(L) Armagh Cathedral
Locks made for the main entrance doors of the Cathedral

Sub-Contractor – IRONMONGERY & METALWORK

Francis Haughey – p. 79
John Sambrook – p. 145

5 JOINERY

Of all building elements windows, doors, their fittings and embellishments can usually tell more of the history of a building than any other. Unfortunately many Georgian terraces, Victorian houses and Edwardian villas have had their picture rails, deeply moulded skirtings and architraves removed, but fashions change and many people now want to restore some of the character of their buildings.

Wood is still the most versatile construction material known and for interior fittings is unsurpassed. Good joiners can make anything from a drawing, a scrap of the original or even a photograph. There are ranges of standard mouldings, in many cases these will be appropriate, but local and regional variation is important and particular mouldings may be specially cut. It is usually not much more expensive to do this particularly when long runs are involved. The scale and proportion of the room should determine the complexity of the mouldings otherwise the joinery becomes grander than the building. For replication purposes examples may be found from other houses of the same period which have not been altered or from museums or photographs. Sometimes details on the outside of the building were replicated inside. Often mouldings were covered up rather than torn out and may be found tucked away under the stairs or in the attic.

Windows deserve a special mention as they are probably the most important factor in the appearance of as building. Timber sliding sash windows, the glazing often divided into small rectangular panes, are the most common traditional window type in Ireland. They look marvellous and give efficient ventilation control and ease of escape in the case of a fire. However, they have a reputation for being draughty and hard to maintain. These problems are exaggerated by salesmen of PVC-U replacements who claim their reproductions look the same and as a result, a rash of replacement windows is sweeping the country. Sometimes thin strips are inserted between two panes of a double glazed unit in an attempt to replicate the pattern of glazing bars, but they fail miserably, fool nobody, are awkward and clumsy, an insult to an old house and stomach turning pastiche in a new one. In addition, there is growing concern over the environmental implications of the use of PVC-U and the toxic waste it can give off in fires.

It is always preferable, and often cheaper, to repair rather than to replace original windows; exact replacements of fine glazing bars and mouldings can be made. Details like the width of frame showing around the window on the outside are of historical importance and should be faithfully matched. Traditional sash windows can be fully draught proofed, easily and inexpensively, with a comprehensive system of brushes and seals. Fitting 'Simplex' sash hinges allow the windows to be cleaned from the inside. In the event of decay, hardwood sections, painted to match the original, can be inserted as in many cases it is only small areas of the sash, usually the cill member, that have decayed.

Weights, sash cords and pulley wheels can be overhauled and replacements are also available. Some very small windows never had weights, instead a piece of wood jammed the sash open. Modern spiral balances are an appropriate replacement in some circumstances but in listed buildings the original system should be replicated.

Leaded windows have also been in use since very early times. In the late eighteenth century some of the simpler forms of leaded windows were copied in cast iron but these forms are rare in comparison to the vertically sliding sash windows.

It is difficult to insert double glazing on small paned sash windows without increasing the size of the glazing bars. Double glazing is the least economic way of insulating a building; it is better to draught seal the windows. Shutters or heavy curtains may be used, radiators placed under windows and an extra layer of insulation added to the roof. Secondary glazing can also be effective and does not destroy the character of a building.

There is an endless variety of traditional door types, both sheeted, and framed and sheeted, or panelled, generally with four or six panels. Some modern 'off the peg' doors are good but others are inappropriate reproductions and have no place in old buildings. Traditional door sizes rarely match 'off the peg' doors and the opening itself should not be changed – the original widths and heights are more important than modern standardisation. Many panelled doors were unnecessarily ripped out, or sheeted over, to improve fire resistance. It is perfectly feasible to upgrade an existing door without losing its character; however the Fire Authority often require test certificates, mainly in public buildings, so new fire resisting panelled doors may have to be made in some instances. Architraves and jamb wall panelling that frame the door should be retained or replicated.

Doors were invariably painted, though they were sometimes grained and the modern preoccupation with natural pine, though attractive, is historically incorrect. External doors, except in the rare cases where they were made from oak, walnut, teak or other exotic woods, must be painted.

External joinery, especially fascias and barge boards, require maintenance and should be made to a high specification if replication becomes necessary. Treated softwood, exterior plywood, hardwood and exterior timber particle boards are all useful and should be painted. Decorative timber barge boards, generally Victorian, are very important features to a building and should be retained.

Finally, the conservation of historic buildings should not be at the expense of the world's forests; all timber used should be specified as coming from a sustainable source. There are difficulties in verifying such claims at present but it is expected that, in the near future, a reliable identification system will be established.

See also   *Section 7 Glass and Glazing – p. 141*
                  Appendix 1: Further reading – p. 199

Sub-Contractor – JOINERY

	Castle Joinery Service 1 Curran Point Larne Co. Antrim BT40 1BS
Telephone:	01574 260422
Contact:	I & L Swan
Size of Firm:	1–10 people Works throughout Ireland
Specialisation:	Manufacture & repair of sliding sash windows Purpose made traditional joinery inc. doors, architraves & panelling
Examples of Work:	(L) Ballyknockan Mill, Carryduff Double hung sash windows with glazing bars, curved and circular headed doors
	ongoing Ulster Folk & Transport Museum Manufacture & repair of double sash windows & reproduction of shop fronts, specialist mouldings
	1998 Private house next to Joymount Arms, Carrickfergus Mahogany double hung sash windows
	1996 Chandlers Bar, Carrickfergus 25 double hung sash windows, 4 staircases, 3 shopfronts, lead lights & glazing

UAHS ref no. 215

Sub-Contractor - JOINERY

Causeway Joinery Manufacturing
92 Main Street
Bushmills
Co. Antrim BT57 8QD

Telephone: 012657 32211   **Fax:** 012657 32211

Contact: John McLean

Size of Firm: 1-10 people
Works throughout Northern Ireland

Specialisation: The combination of traditional craft skills & modern wood-
working technology, with experience of working on churches,
country houses, civic & commercial buildings
Manufacture of standard range of traditional timber sliding sash
windows & panelled doors inc. certificated, hardwood panelled
$^1/_2$ hr. fire doors & frames – The Causeway Hardwood Firedoor –
tested to current regulations & suitable for use in listed buildings
Tailor made, bespoke joinery, inc. replication of original profiles
& mouldings, church & household furniture & fittings

Background: John McLean, Partner - 46 years' experience of construction
industry, on-site & workshop joinery manufacturing, previous
experience of working in timber treatment & rot eradication
Trevor & Gary McLean, Partners - 10 years' on-site & joinery
workshop experience
Company employs own team of qualified joiners

Membership: Member of the Federation of Master Builders

Examples of Work: 1995
(L) Gracehill Golf Club, Stranocum
Sliding sash windows, fire doors & internal joinery
Architect: Caroline Dickson Architects, Londonderry

(L) St Patrick's & St Bridget's Church, Ballycastle
Supply of gothic arch frames, narthex and chapel screens, exterior
& interior doors
Architect: Paddy Byrne, Belfast

1997
New country house, Dervock, Co. Antrim
Sliding sash windows & specialised internal joinery
Architect: Crowther & Co., Carrickfergus

UAHS ref no. 95

1998
Country house, Coleraine, Co. Londonderry
Sliding sash windows & specialised internal joinery
Architect: Fleming, McKernan Associates, Coleraine

127

Sub-Contractor – JOINERY

Dask Timber Products Ltd.
Dublin Road
Loughbrickland
Banbridge BT32 3PB

Telephone: 01762 318696

Fax: 01762 318698
Email: info@dasktimber.co.uk

Contact: David or Stephen Clarke

Size of Firm: 10–50 people
Works throughout Ireland

Specialisation: Manufacture of traditional box sash windows to matching existing profiles, manufacture of box sash windows with double glazing using a special narrow astragal
Design & manufacture of traditional timber conservatories

Background: Manufacturers of purpose made joinery for 25 years

Examples of Work: 1998
Private house, Brookborough
New sliding sash windows in new house
Architect: Manor Architects, Moneymore

1998
Private house, Omagh
New salvaged pitch pine sliding sash windows to a Victorian house
Architect: Arch-Aid, Omagh

1998
(L) College Square, Belfast
All new joinery in renovation of four Georgian townhouses
Architect: Consarc, Belfast

UAHS ref no. 150

Sub-Contractor – JOINERY

O'Neill Bros. (Building Contractors) Ltd.
Site 18
Pennyburn Industrial Estate
L'Derry
Co. Londonderry BT48 0LU

Telephone: 01504 262701   **Fax:** 01504 263215

Contact: Phelim O'Neill

Size of Firm: 50+ people
Works throughout Northern Ireland

Specialisation: Specialist joinery manufacturer, architectural woodcarvings, restoration & refurbishment, church pew manufacturing, stone masons
All types of general construction work

Background: Est. 1956
Experience in all types of restoration work

Membership: Construction Employers Federation N.I., NHBC

Examples of Work: 1998
(L) Parliament Buildings, Stormont, Belfast
Restoration & refurbishment
Reproduced to every detail of the original 1930's architectural —
joinery work
Architect: Consarc Design Group, Belfast

1990
(L) Derry City
Refurbishment & restoration of St Eugenes Cathedral &
construction of new granite built Sacristy & manufacture of oak
pews
Architect: McCormick Tracey Mullarkey, Derry

1986
(L) City Centre, Derry
Five storey interpretation centre (fort)
Traditional built but completely claded in stone to match Derry
City Historic walls
Architect: H M D Architects, Derry

UAHS ref no. 553

Also: Consultant – Quantity Surveyor, Structural Engineer
Sub-Contractor – Stone & Marble, Brick, Leadwork, Joinery, Plasterwork,
Cabinetmaking

Sub-Contractor – JOINERY

Oldtown Joinery
19 Deerpark Road
Bellaghy BT45 8LB
Telephone: 01648 386768   **Fax:** 01648 386768

Contact: Sean Diamond

Size of Firm: 1–10 people
Works throughout Ireland

Specialisation: Traditional box framed windows with full weatherproofing &
brass fittings
Stairs, in both hardwood & softwood made to order
Timber conservatories

Background: 28 years' experience in joinery manufacturing

Examples of Work: 1994
(L) Private house, Tobermore
Manufacture & supply of box framed sliding sash windows to
replace existing
Architect: McCutcheon & Wilkinson, Ballymena

1993
Private houses, Bellaghy
Manufacture, supply & installation of 6 no. new pine staircases
for holiday accommodation
Architect: McCutcheon & Wilkinson, Ballymena

1993
Private house, Stranmillis, Belfast
Restoration in workshop of existing box framed windows, &
manufacture & supply of panelled doors

1993
Private house, Moy
Manufacture & installation of staircase in white oak to new house
Architect: Daly O'Neill & Associates, Portadown

UAHS ref no. 291

130

Sub-Contractor – JOINERY

B Smyth & Son
12 Annacloy Road
Downpatrick
Co. Down BT30 9AE

Telephone: 01396 614085 /
013967 23574

Fax: 013967 23574

Contact: Brian Smyth

Size of Firm: 1–10 people
Works throughout Northern Ireland

Specialisation: Manufacture of purpose made traditional joinery inc. sliding sash windows, doors & stairs
Wood turning & decorative work

Examples of Work: 1989
Public house, Dromara
Refurbishment of bar & lounge with second hand pitch pine joinery
Architect: J D Kelly, Lurgan

1989
(L) Public house, Downpatrick
New staircase
Architect: Taggart MacRandal Partnership, Belfast

1993
Private house, Crossgar
Manufacture & supply of purpose made joinery for restoration & conversion of former mill to dwelling inc. staircase & doors
Architect: Rachel Bevan, Downpatrick

1993
Shop, Ardglass
Manufacture & supply of traditional shop front
Architect: Taggart MacRandal Partnership, Belfast

UAHS ref no. 152

131

Sub-Contractor – JOINERY

Woodmarque Architectural Joinery
25 Mullaghbane Road
Dungannon
Co. Tyrone BT70 1SR

Telephone: 01868 724907 / 723756   **Fax:** 01868 723403

Contact: Brian Quinn or Maurice Craig

Size of Firm: 10–50 people
Works throughout Ireland

Specialisation: Architectural joinery supplied & fitted
Specialised stairs designed
Manufacture of sliding sash windows
Manufacture of internal & external doors
Furniture manufacturer to local based company with world wide
contracts

Background: Years of experience in joinery manufacturing

Membership: Guild of Master Craftsmen

Examples of Work: (L) Temple Bar, Fleet Street, Dublin
Supply of oak windows & doors

1994
(L) House, Northland Road, Dungannon
Sliding sash windows, stairs, fire check doors, architrave,
skirting, mouldings & external doors

(L) 26 Market Street, Dungannon
Double hung sash windows, door frames & interior joinery

1998
(L) St Patrick's School, Donegall Street, Belfast
Restoration and manufacture of gothic style windows and doors

UAHS ref no. 471

132

Sub-Contractor – SASH WINDOWS

Building Services
49 Bessbrook Road
Tullyallen
Mountnorris
Co. Armagh BT60 2DD

Telephone: 01861 507576   **Fax:** 01861 507576

Contact: Noel Cochrane

Size of Firm: 1–10 people
Works in counties Down & Armagh

Specialisation: Refurbishment & repair of existing sash windows, draught proofing, re-cording, new weights & ironmongery etc.
New double or triple glazed, draught proofed, timber sliding sash windows, pre-finished with 'moisture vapour permeable' paint or stain & fitted with dry glazing beads as required – samples of astragal profiles available on request
NIHE approved contractor

Membership: Guild of Master Craftsmen, NHBC warranted builder

Examples of Work: 1996
Private house, Bessbrook
Complete refurbishment of all timber sash windows, including removal & repair of sashes, draught proofing & re-glazing

UAHS ref no. 438

Also: Main Contractor – p. 71

Sub-Contractor – SASH WINDOWS

Cassy Distributors Ltd.
I Bolgers Lane
Kilkeel
Co. Down BT34 4BH

Telephone: 016937 63277   **Fax:** 016937 65453

Contact: P J Hardy

Size of Firm: 1–10 people
Works throughout Northern Ireland

Specialisation: Refurbishment of existing box sash windows, inc. secondary glazing & draught sealing, replacement of pulleys & re-cording, fitting new spiral balances, methods accepted by Environment and Heritage Service – Historic Buildings
Supply & fitting of new box sash windows to traditional patterns
Double glazing fitted to existing casement windows

Background: Company formed 12 years

Membership: Guild of Master Craftsmen
Pilkington 'K' Nationwide Installer

Examples of Work: (L) College Square, Bessbrook

(L) Malone Park, Belfast

5 Coastguard Cottages, Kilkeel

Grange Chapel, Kilkeel – stained glass

Kilkeel Credit Union Building

UAHS ref no. 434

Sub-Contractor – SASH WINDOWS

Ventrolla
I Ardmore Avenue
Ormeau Avenue
Belfast BT7 3HD

Telephone: 01232 646419   **Fax:** 01232 491278

Contact: Tom Lowry

Size of Firm: 1–10 people
Works throughout Northern Ireland

Specialisation: Refurbishment of sliding sash windows
Draught & rattle proofing
Overhauling of sash cords & weights
Installation of window locks & sundry ironmongery

Examples of Work: (L) Private offices, Chichester Street, Belfast
Refurbishment of all sash windows to front façade
Architect: Alastair Coey Architects, Belfast

(L) Private offices, University Square, Belfast
Refurbishment of sash windows to eight houses
Supervising Officer: J Clark & Partners, Belfast

Private house, Hillsborough
Refurbishment of all windows, supplied & fitted new sashes to front

(L) Private house, Draperstown
Refurbishment & overhauling of sash windows

UAHS ref no. 392

135

Sub-Contractor – JOINERY

6 PLASTERWORK AND RENDERS

Until the 1930s lime based plasters were standard and so most old buildings are plastered internally with three coat lime plaster, either directly onto the brick or stone (on the hard) or on horizontal laths on timber framing or joists. The backing coats were generally reinforced with hair or vegetable fibres (fibrous plaster) especially the fine, run (made *in situ*) cornices which were common even in modest buildings. Decorative plasterwork of the eighteenth and nineteenth century can be quite stunning.

Excessive movement in weakening ceiling joists causes cracks, and damp penetration can crumble the surface. Both problems cause the plaster to detach from the laths and eventually fall off. Lath and plaster ceilings and walls are difficult to patch and much fine plasterwork has been lost through lack of timely maintenance. Rot in supporting timbers has long been the excuse for wholesale stripping out of plaster but non-destructive methods are possible combined with the removal of the source of the problem and the insertion, where necessary, of ventilating voids. At the very least cornices and ceiling roses can be securely fixed and repaired in situ.

Cornices, roses and other features are all available as pre-formed mouldings and good plasterers can make up and repair run mouldings. Most fibrous plaster companies can replicate the patterns of cornices and ceiling roses from damaged work or make models from contemporary properties.

For repairs to ordinary, as well as more important historic buildings, plaster made from lime putty and fine sand should be used. In certain circumstances, for example where a wall is very damp, it may, however, be expedient to use a bagged, lime based plaster, such as Limelite from Tilcon which retains some degree of 'breathability' and flexibility after setting.

External renders vary from simple work lined out to resemble stonework, to elaborate stucco pilaster cornices and mouldings. Early examples are in lime based render but by the mid-nineteenth century 'Roman Cement', a naturally occurring clay and lime mix, was the most common material; it is not available today

Renders are subject to thermal stresses and movements in the building fabric. In order to accommodate such movement without cracking and to allow water which is drawn into the fabric to evaporate off, renders, like plasters, should always be lime based. The addition of cement as a guaging material, although common place, is not generally regarded as good conservation practice. In any event, the proportion of cement to lime should not exceed 1:2. If the mix is too cement strong, it will crack, let in water which is unable to escape and eventually detach from the wall.

Many renders contain a stone aggregate. Dry dash, or pebble dash, where the stones are flung on to the wet base coat, is an inappropriate finish for any historic building. A traditional wet dash, where the aggregate is mixed into the render before it is applied to the wall is more suitable. The exact size and type of stone and the texture and colour of the sand used is critical and should be matched to the original work where possible.

Traditional smooth rendered walls, sometimes with 'ashlar' lines marking the 'courses' to resemble stone, were intended to be painted, unless it was already self-coloured by the addition of coloured sands in the render mix.

The successful use of renders and plasters made from lime putty without the addition of cement requires particular skills, both in their specification and their application and after-care on site. Please contact the UAHS for further advice on this subject.

See also   *Appendix 1: Further reading – p. 199*

Sub-Contractor – PLASTERWORK

Andrew Smith & Sean Henderson, Plasterwork
Ballinakill Lodge
Kinnegad
Co. Westmeath

Telephone: 00 353 405 39040   **Mobile:** 086 8199032

Contact: Andrew Smith and Sean Henderson

Size of Firm: 1–10 people
Works throughout Republic of Ireland

Specialisation: Considerable technical skills concerning the development of decorative plasterwork and the appropriate conservation methods. Free hand modelling using lime based technology, for repair, restoration and new work

Background: Both self taught

Examples of Work: 1998
(L) 20 Lower Dominick Street, Dublin
Paint removed from first floor front room using non-alkali paint removers
Architect: Mr Kevin Blackwood, Dublin

1998
12 Hume Street, Dublin
Paint removed from first floor front room using non-alkali paint removers and repair of the plasterwork

1997
113 Lower Baggot Street, Dublin 2
Paint removal and repair to the plasterwork in the principal rooms, staircase and landings, and drawing room ground floor
Architect: Mr T Austin Dunphy

1995
Wood Stock House, Newtown Mount Kennedy, Co. Wicklow
Designed & executed a frieze and copied a cornice from the house for the bar

UAHS ref no. 476

Sub-Contractor – PLASTERWORK

7 GLASS AND GLAZING

Window design developed with technical advances in the production of glass. Early blown glass was replaced by spun glass in the eighteenth century and is still to be found in many historic buildings. It is characterised by irregularities, bubbles and defects. Modern sheet or plate glass, developed by the nineteenth century is largely free from such defects and so is no match for historic glass. Spun glass is becomingly increasingly valuable and period glass is now available; for vernacular buildings agricultural glass may be used.

Nineteenth century float glass allowed larger and more regular panes and simplified glazing patterns. Inexpensive stained glass became available with a range of etched and patterned glasses and was widely used in hall doors, stairs and landings. Stained glass repair is best left to specialist craftsmen. The lead that separates the glass is prone to distortion, sagging and expansion buckling, especially in the larger frames. Sometimes the only solution is complete re-leading although it may be possible to sandwich an old, fragile window between sheets of plain glass. Conservators retain stocks of old glass for repairs.

Modern safety regulations can demand that toughened or laminated glass is used in doors or low windows where a change of use or major renovations require Building Control Approval. This may be too thick for the old mouldings and its greenish colour changes the character. Secondary glazing or internal balustrades may be alternative solutions which preserve the character of the original.

Historically, glass was invariably putty glazed and modern timber slips are inappropriate. For sound insulation internal, secondary glazing is most effective and although inappropriate for fine interiors it does retain the integrity of the original windows.

See also   *Section 5 Joinery p. 123*
         Appendix 1: Further reading – p. 199

Sub-Contractor – GLASS & GLAZING

Art Glass Stained Glass Studio
35 Great James Street
Derry BT48 70S

Telephone: 01504 269369 / 271127   **Fax:** 01504 271127

Contact: Philip Coyle or Sinead Mallow

Size of Firm: 10–15 people
Works throughout Ireland

Specialisation: Restoration, design and manufacturing of:
stained glass, leaded lights, etched glass, bevelled mirrors
Sign writing

Background: Over 14 years' experience of working in stained glass

Membership: British Guild of Stained Glass Artists, NI Guild of Designers

Examples of Work: Restoration & stormglazing of stained glass at:

St Eugene's Cathedral, Derry
Monaghan Cathedral
Magherafelt Parish Church – windows by Mires of Munich
St Matthew's Chapel & St Patrick's Chapel, Belfast
St Macarten's Cathedral, Clogher

New design work at:

Killybegs Parish Church
Malin Head Chapel, Five Finger Strand
St Mary's Chapel, Creggan
St Aidan's Chapel, Bellarena

Restoration of windows by:

Harry Clarke
Mires of Munich
Earley's of Dublin
Clokey's of Belfast

UAHS ref no. 137

142

Sub-Contractor – GLASS & GLAZING

Leadlines and David Esler Stained Glass Studios
54 Whitewell Road
Newtownabbey

Telephone: 01232 775987   **Fax:** 01232 370619

Contact: Eileen or David Esler

Size of Firm: 1–10 people
Works throughout Northern Ireland

Specialisation: Restoration of existing leaded & stained glass
Design & manufacture of new leaded & stained glass for
domestic, ecclesiastical and corporate buildings
Sandblasting design
Protective storm glazing for existing windows

Background: 30 years' experience in stained glass manufacture, design &
fitting. Company Est. 1983

Membership: Federation of Small Businesses

Examples of Work: 1996
(L) St Columba's Church, Knock, Belfast
Manufacture of a new, four light window & tracery based on the
Book of Kells, & the design of Choir Room windows
Architect: A & E Wright, Belfast

Derry City Council Offices
Design & manufacture of window in entrance foyer, presented by
The Honourable The Irish Society
Architect: McCormick Tracey Mullarkey, Londonderry

Antrim Area Hospital
Illuminated stained glass laylight to scanner room

1997
(L) St Cedma's Church, Larne
Design, manufacture & installation of Dean Fair memorial window

1997
(L) Parish Church, Keady
Two, three light windows & tracery 'St Francis feeding the birds'
& 'Christ in glory'

UAHS ref no. 351

1998
(L) Runkerry House, Bushmills
Restoration of Victorian hand painted entrance windows &
interior laylight window

143

Sub-Contractor – GLASS & GLAZING

McNeill – McManus Ltd.
Hydepark
Mallusk
Newtownabbey BT36 8PX

Telephone: 01232 832025 **Fax:** 01232 342317

Contact: Johnathan Neill or Victor Larkham

Size of Firm: 80+ people
Works throughout Northern Ireland

Specialisation: Design & installation of stained glass & leaded windows
Glass embossing
Manufacture of curved glass up to max. 25mm thick,
laminated curved glass & double glazed curved glass units

Background: Company has been producing stained, leaded & embossed
decorative work for 75 years

Membership: Member of NI Division of Glass & Glazier Federation

Examples of Work: 1993
(L) Crown Liquor Saloon, Belfast
Complete replacement of all hand painted & enamelled glass
panels to match original Victorian designs, & acid etched & hand
painted decorative mirrors
Architect: Houston Bell & Kennedy, Belfast

1994
(L) Church, Main Street, Bangor
Repair & reinstatement of stained glass windows
Supervising Officer: James Clark & Partners

1994
(L) Cathedral, Armagh
Complete restoration of two stained glass rose windows
Architect: Leighton Johnston Associates, Belfast

1997
Carlisle Road, Methodist Church, Belfast
Removal, temporary glazing & complete refurbishment of
existing lead light windows
Architect: D Piggot, Crossgar

UAHS ref no. 102

Also manufacture & installation of metal windows – contact G Roy at above address

Sub-Contractor – GLASS & GLAZING

John Sambrook Fanlight Maker
Park House
Northiam
East Sussex TN31 6PA

Telephone: 01797 252615

Contact: John Sambrook

Size of Firm: 1 person
Works throughout Ireland & UK

Specialisation: Manufacture of decorative metal fanlights (including fanlights with lanterns)
Repair of existing metal fanlights
Manufacture of metal roof-lights & windows to 18th century pattern

Background: Greater London Council, Historic Buildings Division 1970–1986
Author of 'Fanlights', pub. Chatto & Windus, 1989

Membership: Fellow of Society of Architectural & Industrial Illustrators
Member of the Association for Study of the Conservation of Historic Buildings

Examples of Work: 1992
(L) Charlemont Square, Armagh
Manufacture of 11 new fanlights to match existing, for the Southern Education & Library Board

1993
(L) Soane Museum, Lincolns Inn Fields, London
Manufacture of new lantern, & repairs to entrance & internal fanlights
Architect: J Harrap Architects, London

1995
(L) Parish Church, Tamlaghtfinlagan
Special metal framework for large stained glass window

1996
(L) 16 Bedford Square, London WC1
New entrance fanlight for Grade I listed building, to match existing at No. 15
Architect: Holloway White Allom Ltd., London

UAHS ref no. 110

Also: Sub-Contractor – Ironmongery & Metalwork

Sub-Contractor – GLASS & GLAZING

Jose Alves-Areias – p. 70
T Chambers & Sons (Enniskillen) Ltd. – p. 74
Ferguson & McIlveen – p. 67

8 TILES AND TILING

Although pounded earth floors were still common in rural vernacular houses until recent times, it is more usual to find slabs of stone, slate, marble and clay 'quarry' tiles laid on ground floors in halls, kitchens and sculleries, with boarded timber floors on joists in the more 'important' rooms and on the upper floors. Original tiled floors add great character to a building, but because they are often laid directly onto the earth, they can be damp and cold. The comfort level can be transformed and the appearance retained by lifting the tiles and re-laying them over a damp proof membrane and rigid insulation on a concrete screed. New and salvaged slate and quarry tiles are available. Laying old tiles may be more costly than putting down modern materials because, like many natural products they may be irregular in shape and thickness but the quality and look of the finished floor should repay this extra effort.

Quarry tiles, which are unglazed, need to be sealed after laying and cleaning to prevent them absorbing stains. The traditional method was to use linseed oil and wax polish. This will make the floor shine but is very labour intensive and a modern cold wax polish is a suitable alternative. Tiled floors should never be treated with any kind of polyurethane coating. This gives a completely inauthentic appearance and may cause the tiles to 'sweat' making for long-term problems by trapping moisture beneath the floor.

The Victorians were fond of small clay floor tiles, commonly laid in complex mosaic patterns, for front halls, hearths, garden paths and churches. They are durable and easy to maintain and should be retained wherever possible. Such geometric tiles are still being made.

Wall tiles have a long history but Victorian mass production, especially for fireplaces ensured widespread popularity. An enormous variety of mouldings and designs created interiors of some opulence in both private and commercial buildings. Wonderful Art Nouveau tiles with stylised plants became common in domestic interiors and new precise reproductions are available.

Old tiles are often very firmly fixed and can easily be broken, so great care is needed when stripping an area for re-use. Rather than replace a large area of original tiles, it may be preferable to repair any broken or damaged ones *in situ*, clean them thoroughly but gently and re-grout.

External tiles made of terracotta or 'faience' were frequently used during the late nineteenth and early twentieth centuries. This material is fragile and easily damaged by clumsy cleaning or repairs and specialist advice should be sought before starting work.

See also   Appendix 1: Further reading – p. 199

Sub-Contractor – TILES & TILING

9 PAINTERWORK

Paint has long been used for the decoration and protection of timber, metal and plaster coatings, and the correct specification is a complex task. Painted surfaces on old buildings will have been built up in many layers and careful stripping back of a small sample area will give clues to a building's decorative history. Caution must be taken when rubbing down old paintwork to avoid inhalation of toxic dust, particularly on timber, because of the former use of lead-based paints. Currently the use of lead paint is restricted by stringent Health and Safety regulations.

Putting together a new, historically correct painting scheme is a specialist task for a major building, but for a building owner wishing to redecorate, the same principles apply:

1   Walls should also be allowed to continue to breathe. If water does penetrate a wall, sealing with 'waterproof' paints will only temporarily mask the problem or make it appear elsewhere. Breathable paints for both internal and external use are available.

2   The quality of a finished scheme relies on thorough preparation of the surfaces – rubbing down, cleaning, stopping and priming. The top coat will not hide deficiencies in the preparation.

3   Choosing the appropriate paint system for the particular material is vital, including the choice of primers.

Internal paint work varies from simple colour washes to highly decorative *tromp l'oeil*. Several commercial companies are now offering a comprehensive range of 'historically accurate' paint colours, but for a very intricate and valuable interior, scientific analysis may be necessary in order to reproduce a colour exactly.

Internal timber surfaces in public buildings may need to be treated to reduce the surface spread of flame. This is achieved by applying approved intumescent paints or stains. The work must be carried out in accordance with the manufacturer's instructions in order to guarantee the system meets the required protection level. The work should also be carried out in relatively warm conditions to avoid clouding the varnish.

See also   *Appendix 1: Further reading – p. 199*

Sub-Contractor – PAINTWORK

10 FITTINGS

Perhaps in Ireland more than elsewhere, the hearth is the traditional centre of the house and even in more modern homes the fireplace is one of the most important architectural features. The fashion in the 1960s and '70s to renovate and modernise, saw chimneys blocked and high quality marble, slate, cast iron and wood fire surrounds discarded. The present owners of many of these house now want to have a real fire and the greatest threat today is the theft and illegal sale of fireplaces to meet a growing demand.

The legitimate salvage trade has however ensured the survival of many of these discarded gems. They are experts at restoring and rebuilding original fireplace surrounds and firebacks, often piecing together broken fragments. They are expensive and will look incongruous in a modern house, but chosen carefully to take account of the age and style of the house and installed correctly, it will add to the value of the property. A good joiner or mason will be able to make a fire surround to fit your requirements exactly and several manufacturers are now producing 'off the peg' ones which may be suitable. The legitimate salvage trade should reveal the source of the fireplace allowing the buyer a clear conscience. Hearths were often slate or stone, again this can be obtained today, often with a metal fender. A dog grate in a firebrick lined recess suits larger rooms, and for smaller rooms, a small fire basket set into a cast iron surround is generally the most appropriate.

Few buildings in Ulster have working external clocks. However, clocks, chimes and bells add a public dimension to a building and where already in place, they should be restored and maintained in working order. Incorporating clocks in new buildings should also be encouraged. Modern technology has replaced labour intensive wind-up pendulums and manually struck bells. There are firms who specialise in the repair and replacement of traditional clocks and for new projects, can offer electronically created chimes and peals.

Interior fittings – the cabinetmakers' skill – are generally outwith the scope of this Directory but occasionally their special skills are used for high quality doors, panelling and fitted furniture in high quality timbers such as walnut, rosewood or maple.

Textile restorers may also be needed to care for fabric panels, curtains and carpets. This is a specialist skill and should not be left to general cleaners.

See also   *Appendix 1: Further reading – p. 199*

Sub-Contractor – CLOCKS & BELLS

J B Joyce & Co. Ltd.
Station Road
Whitchurch
Shropshire SY13 IRD

Telephone: 01948 662817   **Fax:** 01948 665068

Contact: Keith Cotton

Size of Firm: 1–10 people
Works throughout Northern Ireland

Specialisation: Repair, refurbishment & electrification of tower & feature clocks
Manufacture of new clocks & weathervanes

Background: Company has over 100 years' experience of working in Ireland.

Membership: British Horological Institute, Worshipful Company of
Clockmakers, Antiquarian Horological Society

Examples of Work: 1994
Church, Moira, Co Down
Complete overhaul of the clock movement
Architect: G K McKnight, Holywood

1992
Church, Belfast
Restoration of clock dial, re-fitting of carillon machine & fitting
of new clock movement
Architect: G K McKnight, Holywood

1993
Town Hall, Coleraine
Replacement of one dial & restoration of other dials following
bomb damage, refurbishment & cleaning of clock movement

1996
Garvagh War Memorial
Reinstatement of clock movement & hour striking mechanism,
restoration of clock dials

UAHS ref no. 103

Sub-Contractor – ANTIQUE & ARCHITECTURAL RESTORATION

Kelly Antiques
Mullaghmore House
Old Mountfield Road
Omagh
Co. Tyrone BT79 7EX

Telephone: 01662 242314 **Fax:** 01662 250262

Contact: Louis Kelly / Keith Kelly

Size of Firm: 10–50 people
Works throughout Ireland

Specialisation: Restoration of architectural salvage eg. doors, windows & stairs
Restoration of marble, slate & timber fireplace surrounds
Furniture restoration inc. veneering, french polishing & wood carving

Background: Associated with cabinetmaking & bench joinery for five generations

Examples of Work: 1994
Public house, Mellon, Omagh
Furnishing of restaurant & lounge bar

Various hotels, restaurants & public houses
Restoration including Grants Restaurant, Omagh; The Fly, Lower Crescent, Belfast; Manor House Hotel, Killadeas

ongoing
(L) Private house, Omagh
External & internal refurbishment of own 18th century building

UAHS ref no. 380

Sub-Contractor – CABINETMAKING

Castle Glen Joinery Limited
30A Bannonstown Road
Castlewellan
Co. Down BT31 9BQ

Telephone: 013967 78692   **Fax:** 013967 71417

Contact: Edward Ward

Size of Firm: 10–50 people
Works throughout Ireland

Specialisation: Specialist joinery
Design & manufacture of individual items of furniture for private clients
Work mainly in listed buildings or buildings of architectural merit

Background: In business since 1963. Many skilled time served craftsmen

Examples of Work: 1993
Castle in Co. Louth
Design, build and fitting of furniture for two kitchens, bedroom, bathroom, reception room and hall

1994
(L) Private house, Belfast
Fitted furniture and fittings

1997
(L) Private house, Rostrevor, Co. Down
Fitted furniture

1998
Private house, Dublin
Fitted and freestanding furniture for Georgian house

UAHS ref no. 211

See also: Brick and painterwork

Sub-Contractor – CABINETMAKING

Christians of Comber
13 High Street
Comber
Co. Down BT23 5HJ

Telephone: 01247 872690   **Fax:** 01247 872175

Contact: Noel Ludlow

Size of Firm: 1–10 people
Works throughout Northern Ireland

Specialisation: Design & construction of free standing & fitted furniture for kitchens, bedrooms, bathrooms & libraries

Background: 15 years' experience in furniture restoration & 20 years' experience of new & reproduction furniture design

Membership: Kitchen Specialists Association

Examples of Work: Viewing of work in private homes by appointment

UAHS ref no. 161

156

Sub-Contractor – CABINET MAKING

Hugh Drennan & Sons (Cabinet Makers)
Unit 4
278 Killaughey Road
Donaghadee
Co. Down BT21 0LY

Telephone: 01247 820892   **Fax:** 01247 810363

Contact: Hugh Drennan

Size of Firm: 1–10 people
Works throughout Northern Ireland

Specialisation: High class cabinet making

Background: Over 30 years experience in this field. The last 12 years on a full-time basis

Membership: Great Britain Guild of Master Craftsmen
Irish Guild of Master Craftsmen

Examples of Work: 1997
Greyabbey Church of Ireland
Chair to match existing 18th century chair

1993
(L) Armagh Cathedral Library
Map drawers & display cabinets

(L) St Patrick's Church, Ballymena
Panelling in the bell-ringing room

(L) St Patrick's Church, Whitehead
Panelling in the Sacristy

UAHS ref no. 549

Sub-Contractor – CABINETMAKING & JOINERY

The Workshops
1A Lawrence Street
Belfast BT7 1LE
Telephone: 01232 439660

Contact: Martin Carter

Size of Firm: 1–10 people
Works throughout Northern Ireland

Specialisation: Joinery & cabinetmaking using old woods, glass etc.
Use of reclaimed materials in contemporary design
Restoration of furniture & architectural joinery eg. doors,
architraves & panelling
Architectural salvage
Pine stripping

Background: 10 years' experience in the antique business liaising with
architects, building contractors & interior designers

Examples of Work: 1998
Private house, Ravenhill Road, Belfast
Manufacture & installation of pitch pine sliding sash windows
using reclaimed pine

1997
Ruby Tuesdays, Stranmillis, Belfast
Design, manufacture and installation of interior seating, tables
etc., from reclaimed pine. Pitch pine bar made from salvaged pew
Architect: Paddy Byrne, Belfast

1997
Private house, Botanic Court, Belfast
Restoration of staircase, manufacture of table & chairs from local
elm, fitted utility room in teak

Private cottages, Holywood
Staircases in reclaimed pitch pine. Circular windows & frames in
reclaimed timber

UAHS ref no. 403

Also: Supplier - Architectural Salvage

Sub-Contractor – WOODCARVER

Acanthus Woodcarvers
Unit D
Aughrim Lane
Business Park
Stoneybatter
Dublin 7
Eire

Telephone: 00 353 1 8683035   **Fax:** 00 353 1 8683035

Contact: Andrew St Ledger

Size of Firm: 1–10 people
Works throughout Northern Ireland

Specialisation: Specialises in traditional woodcarving eg. carving replica pieces for old furniture; designing contemporary furniture in classical styles for antique surroundings.
Architectural carving. French polishing

Background: Worked with a leading antique dealer and with architects from the Board of Works, who have been involved with preservation work

Membership: Crafts Council of Ireland, state recognition for work

Examples of Work: 1996
(L) Merrion Hotel, Dublin
Conversion of four Georgian houses for hotel, reproduced carvings for newel posts & carved brackets for cut string stairs
Main contractor: John Sisk & Co., Dublin

1992
(L) Old Stand Public House, Wicklow Street, Dublin
Designed a replica hand carved Dutch dresser to match existing 17th century dresser
Main Contractor: David Crowley, Blackrock

1991
(L) O'Brien's Public House, Leeson Street Upper, Dublin
Replacement of hand carved corbels

1988
(L) Dublin Castle
Designed two replica Louis XIV chairs & two additional chairs for dining room as examples of contemporary woodcarving
Main Contractor: Paul Cooke & Board of Works

UAHS ref no. 528

Also: Sub-Contractor – Cabinetmaking

Sub-Contractor – WOODCARVER

Gerald McCormick, Woodcarver
43 Loughmoss Park
Carryduff
Belfast BT8 8PD

Telephone: 01232 813368   **Fax:** 01232 813368

Contact: Gerald McCormick

Size of Firm: 1–10 people
Works throughout Northern Ireland

Specialisation: Church furniture, woodcarving

Background: Time served woodcarving
2 years College of Art
5 years Apprenticeship woodcarving
30 years self-employed

Membership: The Guild of Master Craftsmen

Examples of Work: 1998
(L) Stormont Commons Chamber
Carving egg & dart mouldings, acanthus leaf mouldings (125 metres)

1997
(L) Armagh Court House
Armagh Coat of Arms (4.6 x 3)
Architect: Stephen Leighton MSC RIBA

1996
(L) St Columbas Church, Kings Road, Belfast
New reredos tracery panelling choir frontals made from old pine, two oak chairs & a memorial cabinet
Architect: J McKeown

1996
(L) Montalto House, Ballynahinch
Restoring 18th century fireplace, working on staircase. Making and carving curtain poles
Architect: J J O'Conell

UAHS ref no. 512

Sub-Contractor – WOODCARVER

M Nicholson Wood Carvers
Unit 28, Lisburn Enterprise Centre
Ballinderry Road
Lisburn BT28 2SA

Telephone: 01846 663510   **Fax:** 01846 603084

Contact: Sam Nicholson

Size of Firm: 1–10 people
Works throughout Northern Ireland

Specialisation: Architectural woodcarving

Background: Time served

Examples of Work: 1988
(L) Private buildings, University Road, Belfast
Three pairs of replacement carved corbels to door canopies

1992
Public house, Bradbury Place
Totem pole, 10'6" high x 2' diameter

1994
(L) Private country house, Rostrevor
Carved canopies over bed & window
Interior designer: J Robb, Bangor

1992
Public house, Londonderry
Large carved drinks table & other items

1996
(L) Custom House, Belfast
Carving of replacement capitals & window spirals

UAHS ref no. 342

Sub-Contractor – JOINERY

Philip Steele, Woodcarver
Grays Hill
Bangor
Co. Down BT20 3BB

Telephone: 01247 458675

Size of Firm: 1–10 people
Works throughout Northern Ireland

Specialisation: Carved architectural features, panels, corinthian capitals
Carved newel post & staircase easings & scrolls
Restoration & replication of antique chairs

Background: Trained in London, Gris & Butler; restoration of Chippendale
mirror frames & furniture
Dutch National Trust, Amsterdam; replicating newel posts for
Louis XIV House
Manufacture of church furniture, Grace church work

Membership: Crafts Council of Ireland

Examples of Work: (L) Crown Bar, Great Victoria Street, Belfast
To replace mullions & corinthian capitals on facade of building.
All carved in mahogany
Architect: Mr Mullholland, Houston Bell & Kennedy, Belfast

1989
(L) Hillsborough Castle
Replication of brackets for interior of building, made in reclaimed
pine
Architect: John O'Connell Architects, Dublin

Pearl Assurance House
Pediments made & carved to fit above lift shafts. Design to match
staircase rail
Architect: Roger McMichael, Holywood

Glencairn Hotel, Rostrevor
Replicated easings & hand rail scrolls
Architect: Nugent & McKenna, Armagh

UAHS ref no. 540

162

Sub-Contractor – WALLPAPER PRINTER & CONSERVATOR

David Skinner & Sons
The Mill
Celbridge
Co. Kildare

Telephone: 00 353 1 6272913   **Fax:** 00 353 1 6232780

Contact: David Skinner

Size of Firm: 1–10 people
Works throughout Ireland

Specialisation: Ireland's only specialist wallpaper manufacturer
Produces the 'Great Houses of Ireland' collection containing
eight authentic reproductions of historic Irish patterns
Offers special colourings & a full design & print service for small
print runs

Background: Previously worked as a conservator of historic wallpapers; clients
included the National Trust

Membership: Irish Professional Conservators' & Restorers' Association

Examples of Work: 1998
Library building, King's Inns, Dublin
On-site conservation of mid-nineteenth century wallpaper

1998
Marlay House, Rathfarnham, Dublin
Reproduction of six 18th / 19th century wallpapers discovered as
fragments during restoration of the 18th century house

1996
(L) Armagh Council Chamber, Armagh
Supply of wallpaper for Council Chamber & Committee Room,
for Armagh City & District Council

1993
Kilkenny Castle, Kilkenny
Supply of hand-printed wallpapers copied from original
fragments, for the Office of Public Works

UAHS ref no. 396

Samples of wallpapers are available for a small charge

Sub-Contractor – SPECIALIST PAINTERWORK

Jillian R Forsythe Specialist Paintwork
Mill House
66 Carsonstown Road
Saintfield
Co. Down BT24 7EB
Telephone: 01238 510398

Contact: Jillian Forsythe

Size of Firm: 1–10 people
Works throughout Northern Ireland

Specialisation: Specialist paint techniques eg. ragging, stencilling, sponging, marbling & dragging
Painted murals to commission
Restoration of painted country furniture

Background: BA, work experience with London muralist & furniture restorer

Examples of Work: Temple of the Winds, Mount Stewart
Responsible for complete scheme of specialist redecoration, including painting of ornate plaster ceiling, for the National Trust

Down County Museum
Restoration of items of painted furniture

Retail premises, Belfast
Painted nursery furniture

Show houses, Carryduff
Ragging, stencilling & marbling

UAHS ref no. 388

Sub-Contractor – SIGN WRITER

Brian O'Prey Artist, Designer & Sign Artist
5 Old Movilla Road
Newtownards
Co. Down BT23 8HH
Telephone: 01247 812419

Contact: Brian O'Prey

Size of Firm: 1–10 people
Works throughout Northern Ireland

Specialisation: Typeface, art & corporate identity design
Painting, hand lettering & gilding of traditional and contemporary
timber signs, also wall & aluminium signs & pictorials
Design & reproduction of camera ready artwork for printing

Background: Self employed for 15 years, four generations of family engaged in
sign writing
Study of historic typefaces and signage

Membership: Corporate member of the Guild of Master Craftsmen

Examples of Work: 1996
Ulster American Folk Park, Omagh
Design & execution of late 19th – early 20th century signage &
showcards for television advertisement, including research of
appropriate typefaces and colours

1996
(L) Presbyterian Church, The Square, Comber, Co. Down
Restoration of 150 year old clock face & hands, and gilding of
numerals & hands as original

1996
Karlsruhe, Germany
Painting & signwriting of traditional 'Irish' signs (executed in
Newtownards workshop)

1996
(L) The Royal Hotel, Bangor, Co. Down
Design & supply of hanging bracket & production of painted &
gilded heraldic shields

UAHS ref no. 187

165

Sub-Contractor – CABINETMAKING

Acanthus Woodcarvers – p. 159
William Dowling Ltd. – p. 75
Joseph McClune – p. 82
O'Neill Bros. (Building Contractors) Ltd. – p. 129

Sub-Contractor – WOODCARVING

B Smyth & Son – p. 131

11 REMEDIAL WORKS

Building repair technology has become increasingly complex in recent years and there is a confusing array of specialist systems designed to counteract rot, decay and damp. In many cases though, the temptation is to go for a technical solution when perhaps more basic, common-sense methods may be less destructive to the building's fabric and occupants and equally effective. Retention of the maximum amount of original fabric must always be the guiding principal. Good remedial specialists should recommend the best system for each individual problem, but a few general guidelines may be useful.

Damp proof courses are rare in old buildings, although a layer of slate or bitumen is sometimes seen running through the wall. Rising damp is often caused when the ground level outside the building is above the floor level inside and dampness is able to penetrate through the walls. Lowering the ground level and providing an external 'french' drain, a perforated pipe laid in a gravel bed around the building to take away excess surface water, and putting in vents to allow ventilation under suspended timber floors will generally alleviate the problem. Gentle background heating inside the house will help to dry out the walls. Most injected chemical DPCs will only work on narrow brick walls. A typical rubble stone wall has voids and rubbish in its core and an injected DPC cannot form a continuous barrier, although specialist grouts are available for filling larger voids. Many old buildings have survived for hundreds of years without a damp proof course but if it is deemed necessary, the best option is an electro-osmotic system, where a titanium wire carrying a very low electric voltage is chased into the plaster around the external walls. Results can be variable on very thick walls, but it is by far the least disruptive method and does not introduce potentially damaging chemicals into the fabric of the building.

Treatment for dry rot, woodworm and other fungal and insect attack is another controversial area. The discovery of dry rot in particular is often accompanied by panic and hysteria. The injection of large quantities of toxic materials and hasty over-zealous remedial work has resulted in the loss of many fine interiors. Dry rot will only survive in damp, warm conditions where there is little air movement, in badly ventilated floor voids and behind window shutters for example. If the source of the water is removed and the ventilation of fresh air improved the dry rot will die. There are few experts who will adopt such a studied yet simple approach. Insurance premiums and demands of mortgage companies often lead to radical stripping out of wholly unaffected timber and plaster which may well be unnecessary. A general change of attitude is long overdue. Good maintenance is the best remedy – gutters should be kept free of leaves and debris, broken downpipes and overflows repaired and pointing and flashings, especially on flat roofs and in hidden valleys should be checked regularly. Wet rot and woodworm are easily eradicated without great loss of original fabric.

Repairs to chimneys can sometimes seem a black art rather than a scientific process. Flues in old houses were rarely lined and often roof timbers were built into the chimney breast and exposed to smoke. Over the years these can become charred and in some instances can smoulder without detection. This is one of the commonest causes of fires in old buildings, especially if modern closed high output fires burning high temperature smokeless fuel are introduced. This type of fire and 'coal effect' gas fires must always have a lined flue. Inserting a flue liner into an old chimney and filling the voids with insulating material can be a dirty and awkward job and is best left to an expert. Even if the flue stays unlined for an open fire, it is sensible to remove built in timbers, especially in thatched houses.

Large chimneys are divided into multiple flues which are separated from each other by thin brick divisions called 'feathers'. Flue gases gradually eat away at the brick and can cause the 'feathers' to crack and eventually collapse, blocking a flue or opening a smoke passage from one flue to the next. Bird's nests, accumulated soot and broken 'feathers' can combine to block or even destroy a chimney. Tell tale signs are smoke coming out of more than one chimney pot when only one fire is lit or smoke coming out of one fireplace when the only fire lit is in the room next door. Coal that is not being burnt correctly in a closed fire will produce invisible and highly toxic flue gases of odourless carbon monoxide which can spread throughout the house if left unchecked. It is always a wise precaution to have chimneys swept annually and to consult a 'chimney doctor' or the Coal Advisory Service if you are lighting fires for the first time or are aware that there might be a problem.

If it is necessary to rebuild a chimney, the original corbelled courses around the top should be replicated and either the old pots or matching new pots reinstated. Excellent reproductions of traditional terracotta pots are available. Redundant flues must be fitted with a ventilated cap to the pots and a grille built into the chimney breast to prevent damp and condensation. Even unused chimneys add great presence to a house and the temptation to demolish them when the central heating is installed should be resisted.

See also   *Appendix 1: Further reading – p. 199*

Sub-Contractor – REMEDIAL WORKS

DANLOR Services Ltd.
52 Adelaide Avenue
Belfast BT9 7FY

Telephone: 01232 382820   **Fax:** 01232 382821

Contact: David Boyd & Dan McCaffrey

Size of Firm: 10–50 people
Works throughout Ireland

Specialisation: Remedial & Restoration
Environmental control of rot & timber infestation
Minimum use of chemicals
Cost sensitive
Survey, specification & construction
Specialist period contractors

Background: Qualifications of staff: BSc. Civil Engineering, BSc. Building, MCIoB

Membership: Chartered Institute of Building

Examples of Work: 1995
(L) Newry Cathedral
Structural repairs to roof, re-slating, leadwork & treatment for rot
– acted as main contractor
Architect: McLean & Forte, Belfast

1996
(L) Church, Carrickfergus
Major restoration inc. dry rot treatments, repairs to walls, structural timbers & ornamental plaster moulding, & introduction of monitoring system – acted as main contractor
Architect: Knox & Maxwell, Bangor

1997
12 College Square North, Belfast
(L) Major renovation including dry rot treatment and damp proofing – acted as main contractor
Architect: Mackel & Dogherty, Belfast

1998
185 Ormeau Road, Belfast
Eradication of damp and rot. Renewal of cavity wall ties
Architect: Philip Lynn

UAHS ref no. 357

Also: Consultant – Building Defects & Remedial Works, fibrous moulding & installation of cavity wall ties. Main Contractor.

Sub-Contractor – REMEDIAL WORKS

McCleery Mathison Ltd.
Unit 3, East Bank Road
Carryduff
Belfast BT8 8BD

Telephone: 01232 815070   **Fax:** 01232 815046

Contact: Raymond McCleery

Size of Firm: 1–10 people
Works throughout Northern Ireland

Specialisation: Treatment of building timbers against attack by wood boring insects or wood rotting fungi
Installation of damp proof courses including replastering and ancillary works
Basement tanking systems

Background: Dermot Mathison – Certificate of the Institute of Wood Science
Ray McCleery – previous employment as surveyor with major timber treatment company
Both have over twenty-five years experience in the timber treatment industry

Membership: Guild of Master Craftsmen, UAHS

Examples of Work: Remedial works & treatments at the following locations:

1993
(L) Downshire Arms Hotel, Hilltown, Co. Down
Architect: Patrick O'Hagan & Associates, Newry

1994
(L) Town Hall, Bangor

1994
(L) Court Street, Newtownards
Architect: Hearth, Belfast

1995/96
(L) Custom House, Belfast
Architect: John Neil Partnership, Belfast

1997/98
(L) Runkerry House, Bushmills
Architect: Halliday, Fisher & Munroe

UAHS ref no. 450

Sub-Contractor – CHIMNEYS

Chimcoat (NI) Limited
40B The Cutts
Derriaghy
Dunmurray
Belfast BT17 9HN

Telephone: 01232 611229   **Fax:** 01232 611439

Contact: H H McKinty or B M Hamill

Size of Firm: 1–10 people
Works throughout Northern Ireland

Specialisation: Survey & report on the condition of flues and chimney stacks including CCTV of the internal condition of flues, demolition & rebuilding of stacks, relining of flues

Background: More than 45 years spent in the building industry
30 years as Director of Coal advisory service and Director of British Coal contracts in NI
Specialist contractors registered with NIHE with approvals for flue testing, chimney reaming & descaling and 'chimcoat' lining systems

Membership: Member of Institute of Domestic Heating and Environmental Engineers, Guild of Master Craftsmen

Examples of Work: 1998
(L) Runkerry House, Bushmills
The relining of 12 flues – some 14m high
Architect: Halliday Frazer Munro

1998
(L) 20 Moira Road, Hillsborough
The relining of five flues and building in of cast iron antique fireplaces

1997
(L) 11 The Square, Hillsborough
Relining of flue from basement through four storey's

1997
Bellevue House, Killowen Old Road, Rostrevor
Relining of all flues
Architect: Gibben & Donaghy, Armagh

UAHS ref no. 545

Sub-Contractor – CHIMNEYS

Thermocrete (N.I.)
43a Tates Avenue
Belfast BT9 7BY

Telephone: 01232 663641 **Fax:** 01232 662832

Contact: Ian Montgomery

Size of Firm: 10–50 people
Works throughout Northern Ireland

Specialisation: Pumped lining of flues. Rebuilding decorative external stacks
General chimney works, traditional chimney lining
General plumbing work

Background: 20 years plumbing and heating contractor
10 years flue lining contractor

Membership: Builders guarantee scheme. Ceramics Institute

Examples of Work: 1997
(L) Baronscourt, Omagh
9 flues relined by pumping thermocrete

ongoing
£300,000 flue lining works p.a. for NIHE

1998
(L) Killyleagh Castle, County Down
Reline flue for oil fired boiler

(L) Glenalla House, Claudy
Reline flue

UAHS ref no. 564

Also: Sub-Contractor – Plumber

Sub-Contractor – REMEDIAL WORKS

12 SERVICES

The introduction of any new services into an old building demands skill and sensitivity. Considerable ingenuity is required to conceal pipe and cable runs to avoid damaging plaster cornices and skirtings whilst allowing for regular maintenance and access if something does go wrong. Carefully chosen positions for service entry points, soil vent pipes, over-flows and internal fittings such as smoke detectors, radiators and electrical sockets can make all the difference to the visual success of a project. In old buildings this is usually best worked out on site in collaboration with the builder or contractor.

Time and care should be taken in choosing new light fittings, electrical switches and sockets. In the absence of any original light fittings, which could be repaired or matched, these can be either reproduction or modern. Both types can be appropriate, although many off the shelf 'period' fittings are poorly designed. Well made, authentic reproductions are available, but they can be expensive and in many cases, small, discreet modern lights will be more sympathetic to an interior than ornate reproductions. It is possible to adapt brass 'dolly' light switches to modern standards when re-wiring but generally sockets should be replaced and simple, plain fittings are to be preferred. Indirect, diffused lighting is often kinder to old interiors, and early houses which did not have gas or electric lighting may be best respected by using table lamps. Wall lights can avoid damaging delicate or decorated ceilings.

Installing central heating into historic buildings can create problems; drying out timber which leads to panelling and doors warping and causing excessive moisture to be drawn through walls. The absorption and evaporation of water in and out of an old building is generally in a state of balance, this is what is meant by a building 'breathing'. Introducing a new system can upset this equilibrium and central heating should always be used sparingly at first to allow the building to slowly warm up and readjust itself. If extensive restoration is being undertaken, an under floor heating system may be the solution for an early building where radiators would not be appropriate. Second-hand or new cast iron column radiators suit later buildings and decorative radiator cases can be used to advantage.

Thatched buildings must be kept dry all year round and a system of background heating, such as storage radiators should be considered if the building is only used sporadically.

Satellite dishes are totally out of place on historic buildings and indeed putting a dish on a listed building requires Listed Building Consent. Television aerials should be positioned in attics.

It is traditional, through expediency rather than design, to run the electricity supply into a building along the eaves, but in general the common tangle of wires, especially in urban areas, bringing services into a building can mar its appearance and all efforts should be made with NIE and BT to have the cables put underground.

The introduction of complex security systems into historic buildings and compliance with Building Control regulations regarding fire safety and means of escape will often pose difficult problems. Conditions on the Building Control Approval can be amended or waived in certain circumstances and it is always sensible to discuss these issues on site with the official concerned. Most requirements can met with willingness and imagination.

See also   *Appendix 1: Further reading – p. 199*

Services & Utilities – ELECTRICIAN

I C D Electrical
6 New Road
Donaghadee
Co. Down BT21 0DR
Telephone: 01247 882570

Contact: Sam Beck

Size of Firm: 1–10 people
Works throughout Northern Ireland

Specialisation: Electrical installation: industrial, commercial, domestic with particular attention to the period of the building

Background: Approved by Joint Industry Board (Electrical Contractors)

Membership: NGCEGC, IIB Approved Contractor

Examples of Work: Ulster Folk & Transport Museum
Period street lighting

(L) Ulster Folk & Transport Museum
Refurbishment of lighting at Manor House

UAHS ref no. 85

Sub-Contractor – ELECTRICIAN & PLUMBER

13 SPECIALIST SURVEYS & PHOTOGRAPHY

An accurate and appropriate survey of any building is the basis for informed decision-making on a project and is usually the first step in establishing the nature and extent of the work required. Surveys range from simple recording in plan, section and elevation, to highly technical, non-destructive techniques to locate hidden problems.

For most buildings, a traditional, measured survey will be sufficient but care must be taken not to overlook important details. Few old buildings are true and square, and it should not be assumed that rooms are perfectly rectangular – a series of diagonal measurements will give an accurate picture of the real shape of the spaces, both internally and externally. When extensive work is planned, it is important to record the size, shape and location of all interior fittings such as skirtings, architraves, dadoes, cornices and other mouldings. Once demolitions commence it is more than easy to forget where exactly such items belong: labelling each piece of joinery as it is taken down helps to prevent mistakes later.

Rectified, or corrected photography can be a valuable tool for recording the elevations of large and complex buildings. At its most refined, this technique is called photogrammetry, where the photographic information is stored on a computer disc and used to generate highly accurate drawings in two or three dimensions.

Other tools, such as X-ray, infra-red and ultra-sound can be used to detect hidden problems such as voids or corroded metal fixings within the fabric of the building itself. The most common are magnet-based 'cover meters' and impulse radar. The successful use of these techniques requires specialist advice, and they are normally only employed on the most intricate and important of structures where the high cost can be justified. However, such costs may be offset by the early identification of problems before they become serious defects, requiring major intervention to remedy.

Access for surveying is often a problem and the cost of scaffolding can greatly outweigh the cost of the survey. Mobile hoists are in general use, but for very awkward buildings, roped access techniques are often more effective, allowing even the most hidden parts of a building to be thoroughly investigated and recorded.

Sub-Contractor – PHOTOGRAMMETRIC SURVEYS

B K S Surveys
47 Ballycairn Road
Coleraine BT51 3HZ

Telephone: 01265 52311   **Fax:** 01265 57637
                                       Email: sales@bks.co.uk

Contact: Niamh O'Hagan or John McNally

Size of Firm: 50+ people
Works throughout Britain & Ireland

Specialisation: Close range photogrammetry producing scaled line images of building elevations
Services include architectural surveys (plans, sections & elevations); recording of historic monuments; structural monitoring & inspection of buildings; site surveys

Background: Experience of working with private, public & corporate bodies

Membership: The Survey Association, the Photogrammetric Society, National Computing Council

Examples of Work: 1990
(L) Florence Court, Co. Fermanagh
Photography & production of 1:50 scale drawings of elevations, & production of AutoCAD digital data
Architect: A & E Wright, Belfast

1989
(L) Castle Ward, Strangford
Photography & production of 1:50 scale models of elevations
Architect: Denis Piggot, Crossgar

1992
(L) Town Hall, Coleraine
Detailed survey of fabric following bomb damage, photography & production of 1:100 drawings & full-size details in AutoCAD format for 2D & 3D reproduction
Architect: W & M Given Architects, Coleraine

1996
(L) Rievaulx Abbey, North Yorkshire
Photography, control & photogrammetric plotting to produce 1:20 scale drawings of all elevations, final 3D AutoCAD data & set of mono A4 size B/W prints, for English Heritage

UAHS ref no. 374

Sub-Contractor – ARCHITECTURAL PHOTOGRAPHY

Christopher Hill Photographic
17 Clarence Street
Belfast BT2 8DY

Telephone: 01232 245038   **Fax:** 01232 231942
Email: ChrisHillPhotographic@btinternet.com

Contact: Christopher Hill

Size of Firm: 1–10 people
Works throughout Northern Ireland

Specialisation: All photography & print related work
Extensive photographic library

Background: 18 years as a professional photographer, working with
'Architect's Journal', 'Architectural Review' & 'Perspective'
magazine
Work with award winning architectural practices

Membership: Institute of Chartered Designers

UAHS ref no. 366

Also: Consultant – Photographer

Sub-Contractor – DIFFICULT ACCESS SPECIALIST

Rope Access Specialists
Newtate
Enniskillen
Co. Fermanagh BT92 1FW

Telephone: 01365 348443   **Fax:** 01365 348081
Email: ropeaccessspecialists@CompuServe.com

Contact: Tim Fogg

Size of Firm: 1–10 people
Works throughout Ireland

Specialisation: The use of industrial rope techniques in place of traditional access systems to work safely at height or in difficult / restricted locations to carry out photographic and structural surveys, cleaning, maintenance and light repairs

Background: Experience in last 9 years in difficult access work according to standard practices & safety procedures
Teams use mandatory back-up systems and are qualified to internationally recognised standards

Membership: Industrial Rope Access Trade Association

Examples of Work: 1990
Castle Coole, Co. Fermanagh
External photographic & visual survey of external elevations, for the National Trust

1994
Belfast Institute of Further & Higher Education, College Square
Structural & photographic survey of west elevation
Consulting Engineers: Kirk McClure Morton, Belfast

1997
Dublin City Hall
Maintenance & cleaning of stained glass panels in the dome for Dublin Corporation

1998
Lincoln Building, Belfast
Interior & exterior maintenance & cleaning for DoE Construction Service

UAHS ref no. 109

179

SUPPLIERS

Supplier – STONE & OTHER BUILDING MATERIALS

David Scott (Agencies) Ltd.
7–19 Blythe Street
Belfast BT12 5HU

Telephone: 01232 232136   **Fax:** 01232 438611

Contact: David Scott

Product Details: Goods / materials supplied throughout Northern Ireland

Specialisation: Supply of sandstone, limestone, marble, granite, terrazzo, terracotta & slate
Architectural ironmongery
Architectural salvage
Ceramic tiles for walls & floors

Technical Literature: Free brochure & tariffs

Technical Advice: Free technical advice
Full design service charged on a fee basis

UAHS ref no. S 6

Supplier – SLATES, TILES & BRICKS

CAPCO Roofing Centre
27 Balmoral Road
Belfast BT12 6QA

Telephone: 01232 662535   **Fax:** 01232 662505

Contact: Colin McClelland

Goods / materials supplied throughout Northern Ireland

Product Details: Sole authorised Northern Ireland supplier of new Penrhyn 'Bangor Blue' slates, also Westmoreland, Welsh, Spanish & North American slates to BS 680
'Dreadnought', 'Keymer' & 'Tuiles Lambert' large format clay tiles
'Redbank' ornamental ridge tiles & fittings
'York' handmade bricks & paviors
Suppliers of imperial size bricks for renovation work

Technical Literature: Free brochure & product details

Technical Advice: Free advice service

UAHS ref no. S 54

182

Supplier – TRADITIONAL BRICKS

Lamb's Bricks & Arches
Nyewood Court
Brookers Road
Billingshurst
West Sussex RH14 9RZ

Telephone: 01403 785141   **Fax:** 01403 784663

Contact: Jonathan Lamb

Goods / materials supplied throughout Northern Ireland

Product Details: Specialist brickmakers for 100 years
Manufacture & supply of three stock ranges of bricks from three
UK brickworks, in ten imperial sizes & fifteen colours, inc. red
rubber, yellow rubber, mixed gault & Mulberry stocks
Sole manufacture of traditional TLB red rubber material, or
'cutting blocks' for use in matching historic brickwork
Production of specials, inc. guaged arches, special profiles &
carved work

Technical Literature: Company literature pack supplied free of charge to architects,
contractors & clients

Technical Advice: Free advice given on the suitability of different types of brick &
stone for conservation projects & new build, including
recommendations for mortar mixes
Full design service, inc. site visits & preparation of full size
UAHS ref no. S 52   working drawings & sketch layouts

Supplier – LIME PUTTY

Clogrennane Lime Ltd.
Clogrennane
Co. Carlow

Telephone: 00 353 503 31811   **Fax:** 00 353 503 31607

Contact: Leo Grogan or Larry Byrne

Goods / materials supplied throughout Northern Ireland

Product Details: High quality lime putty in 25kg round tubs
Quick lime
Hydrated lime

Technical Literature: Free instruction leaflets for making lime mortars, plasters &
UAHS ref no. S 287   limewashing

Supplier – LIME PUTTY, MORTARS & LIMEWASHES

Narrow Water Lime Service
Newry Road
Warrenpoint
Co. Down BT34 3LE

Telephone: 016937 53073   **Fax:** 016937 53073

Contact: Dan McPolin

Goods / materials supplied throughout UK & Ireland

Product Details: Lime putty produced on site from Kilwaughter limestone burnt with solid fuel in traditional kiln & sold in plastic tubs
Ready mixed coarse stuff (mortars for building & pointing) in a range of colours & aggregate mixes
Plain & pigmented limewash
Carbonated water (for consolidation of decayed limestones)
Flints
Analysis of historic mortars & replication of material for building, pointing, renders & interior plasterwork

Technical Literature: Free brochure & price list
Participants in practical workshops (see p. 52) are given full range of supporting material

Technical Advice: Free telephone advisory service, customers are also encouraged to visit the premises at Narrow Water
Mortar analysis & consultancy services are charged on a fee basis

UAHS ref no. S 46

Also: Consultant – Dan McPolin at Narrow Water Lime Service, Historic & Traditional Building Consultancy & Training – p. 52

Supplier – HYDRAULIC LIME & LIME PRODUCTS

Telling Lime Products Ltd.
Primrose Avenue
Fordhouses
Wolverhampton WV10 8AW

Telephone: 01902 789777   **Fax:** 01902 398777

Contact: Jeffrey Parmley for local Northern Ireland agent

Goods / materials supplied throughout Ireland

Product Details: Natural hydraulic lime (i.e. lime with a natural set), supplied either as a dry hydrate for blending on site with local aggregrates or pre-mixed & bagged for renders, grouts, mortars & plasters in a wide range of colours & textures
Various strengths of hydraulic set are available

Supply of lime based paints in over ninety shades & colours
Marmalux polished marble finishes

All materials are warranted by indemnity insurance up to £500,000

Technical Literature: 'Unilit' technical literature giving full details of hydraulic lime products inc. coverages
'Cori' paint brochure giving full details of colours & applications

Technical Advice: Site visits, analysis of materials & specifications

UAHS ref no. S 50

Supplier – CHIMNEY POTS etc.

Ulster Fireclays Limited
Washingbay Road
Coalisland
Co. Tyrone BT71 5EG

Telephone: 01868 740436   **Fax:** 01868 747430

Contact: Hugh Cullen, Brendan Brankin

Goods / materials supplied throughout Northern Ireland

Product Details: Manufacture of clay products:
flue linings, air bricks, ridge tiles, drainage channels and quarry tiles
Can supply items required for the refurbishment of old and listed buildings, hand making being a speciality
Member of the Clay Pipe Development Association Limited

Technical Literature: Free brochures and product details

Technical Advice: Free technical advice

UAHS ref no. S 31

Supplier – RAINWATER GOODS

D Alexander Builders Providers
136–210 Tennant Street
Belfast BT13 3GF

Telephone: 01232 751756   **Fax:** 01232 352807

Contact: David Alexander

Goods / materials supplied throughout Northern Ireland

Product Details: Cast iron & cast aluminium rainwater systems

Technical Advice: Free advisory service on choice of components
Design service for non-standard products

UAHS ref no. S 13

186

Supplier – RAINWATER GOODS & IRONMONGERY

James E Ball Ltd.
143 Northumberland Street
Telephone: Belfast BT13 2JN
01232 327752   **Fax:** 01232 241003

Contact:
G Warwick

Goods / materials supplied throughout Northern Ireland
Product Details:
Cast iron rainwater pipes, gutters & fittings
Full range of architectural ironmongery inc. locks
Sheet lead
Technical Literature:
Free brochure of product details

Technical Advice:
Free advice service

UAHS ref no. S 16

Supplier – RAINWATER GOODS

J & J Longbottom Limited
Bridge Foundry
Holmfirth
Huddersfield
West Yorkshire HD7 1AW
Telephone: 01484 682141   **Fax:** 01484 681513

Contact: S R Brook

Goods / materials supplied throughout Northern Ireland

Product Details: Cast iron rainwater & soil goods, inc. pipes, gutters, ornamental heads, air bricks & ancillary ironwork

Technical Literature: 40 page, fully illustrated catalogue of traditional cast iron rainwater & soil goods available free on request

Technical Advice: Free advice on all products

UAHS ref no. S 35

Supplier – METAL RAINWATER GOODS

P F C Rainwater Systems Ltd.
Unit 11
Loughside Industrial Estate
Dargan Crescent
Belfast BT3 9JP

Telephone: 01232 781830   **Fax:** 01232 781270

Contact: Martin Brown

Goods / materials supplied throughout Ireland

Product Details: Manufacture of specialist, metal rainwater systems, copying existing profiles
Manufacture of new systems to match architects' details
Supply of bespoke hopper heads & ornamental cast iron goods

Technical Literature: Free technical literature & specifications

Technical Advice: Comprehensive free service
Gutter sizing & site measurement
Provision of samples
Sourcing of bespoke rainwater goods

UAHS ref no. S 47

Full fitting service available

Supplier – FOUNDRY CASTINGS

Ulster Castings Limited
2–4 Bridge Street
Comber
Newtownards
Co. Down BT23 5AT

Telephone: 01247 872372   **Fax:** 01247 870088

Contact: Jim Needham BSc. MIBF

Goods / materials supplied throughout UK & Ireland

Product Details: Manufacture of specialised, gravity die castings in aluminium alloys to standard or special design
Architectural hardware eg. gratings & ventilators
Components for glazing systems, inc. window ironmongery
Components for furniture manufacture & repair
Epoxy powder painting
CNC milling & general machining in all materials

UAHS ref no. S 45

Technical Literature: Free company brochure available on request

Technical Advice: Full design service

Supplier – STEEL & WROUGHT IRON COMPONENTS

John H Place (Steels) Ltd.
44 Blackpark Road
Toomebridge
Co. Antrim BT41 3SL

Telephone: 01648 50481 or   **Fax:** 01648 50175
07000 564675

Contact: Derek F Place

Goods / materials supplied throughout Northern Ireland

Product Details: Engineering bar steel, high tensile steels, chrome plated bar etc.
Wrought iron decorative components, such as twisted bars,
rosettes, collars, profile strip, handrails, scrolls & railheads for
gates, railings, window grilles, balustrades, fencing etc. – with
other components available to order from Italian manufacturers
Weathervanes & components
Supply of new cast iron finials from samples to match existing
railings

Note:
Supply of components only – but can recommend suitable
fabricators

Technical Literature: Comprehensive 400 page catalogue £35 + p&p £4
Design book £15 + p&p
Abridged handbook £1.50 + p&p £1
Some leaflets free of charge

Technical Advice: Assistance provided with selection of suitable components. We
also endeavour to source items not included in our current range.
List of fabricators, regionalised according to postcodes can be
provided free for those customers not wishing to fabricate the
components themselves.

UAHS ref no. S 5

Supplier – GLASS

The London Crown Glass Company Ltd.
21 Harpsden Road
Henley-on-Thames
Oxfordshire RG9 1EE

Telephone: 01491 413227   **Fax:** 01491 413228

Contact: Christopher Salmond

Goods / materials supplied throughout Northern Ireland

Product Details: Period window glass
Handblown cylinder sheet glass in stock & cut sizes
Georgian sheet glass in stock & cut sizes
Genuine sheet glass in stock & cut sizes

Technical Literature: Free brochure, tariff & information sheet

Technical Advice: Free service – travelling costs are charged where necessary
Identification of old window glass by method of manufacture, for
replacement or recording purposes eg. insurance
Illustrated talk on the history of glass
Full details of our range of period glass, together with a history
and description of window glass manufacturer can be found on
the Internet: www.londoncrownglass.co.uk

UAHS ref no. S 1

Supplier – SPECIALIST PAINTS, MATERIALS & EQUIPMENT

Jocasta Innes Paint Magic
59 High Street
Holywood
Co. Down BT18 9AQ

Telephone: 01232 421881   **Fax:** 01232 421823

Contact: Patricia James

Goods / materials supplied throughout Northern Ireland & the Republic of Ireland
24 hour delivery service available – prices on application

Product Details: Full range of specialist paints & equipment, inc. colourwash, woodwash, liming paste & crackleglaze, traditional & modern varnishes, shellac & other decorative materials
Ready-mixed soft distemper in white & 5 tinted shades
Standard range of matt & silk emulsions in 12 colours, developed in collaboration with Craig & Rose
Agents for lead based paints, manufactured by Craig & Rose – paint manufacturers to the Royal Palaces, for use under regulation on Grade A listed buildings – paint scrape analysis also available
Lime putty & pigments for mixing

Paint Magic organises a full range of workshops in specialist paint techniques, including wall effects, covering the use of soft distemper, & mixing lime putty & tinting using natural pigments – full details & prices on application

Technical Literature: Full range of literature inc. mail-order catalogue, colour charts & paint samples
The shop stocks books on decorating techniques, furniture painting etc.

Technical Advice: Advisory service
Design & decoration service available for both restoration & new build projects

UAHS ref no. S 57

Also: Sub-Contractor – Specialist Paintwork

Supplier – TRADITIONAL PAINTS

Potmolen Paint
27 Woodcock Industrial Estate
Warminster
Wiltshire BA12 9DX

Telephone: 01985 213960   **Fax:** 01985 213931

Contact: Gillian Butcher

Goods sent from works via carrier throughout Ireland and the UK

Product Details: Traditional & natural paints & coatings for traditional buildings inc. distempers, linseed oil primers & glosses
Lime putty required for limewashing & mortars

Technical Literature: Free brochure, tariff, colour chart & information sheets

Technical Advice: Free telephone advice

UAHS ref no. S 2

Supplier – PAINTS & COATINGS

Rustins Ltd.
Waterloo Road
Cricklewood
London NW2 7TX

Telephone: 0181 450 4666   **Fax:** 0181 452 2008

Contact: Henry Davis National Sales Manager

Sole distributors for Northern Ireland
John Frackelton & Sons Ltd.
25 Imperial Drive
Belfast BT6 8JH
Tel: 01232 732231
Contact: W McCartney Sales Director

Product Details: Manufacturers of an extensive range of specialist paints, wood finishes, stains & floor finishes
Traditional products inc. Button polish, French polish, linseed oil & 'Strypit' paint & varnish remover

Technical Literature: Instructions are supplied with all products
Additional technical information available on request

UAHS ref no. S 22

Supplier – TRADITIONAL & MODERN RADIATORS

Telephone:

B M Heat Services / The Radiator Shop
111 South Street
Newtownards
Co. Down BT23 4JU
01247 813460 /   **Fax:** 01247 819909
815991

Contact:

Paul McCulla

Product Details:

Goods / materials supplied throughout Northern Ireland

Suppliers of new cast iron, steel & aluminium radiators in
traditional & modern styles
Also agents for
Walney 'Victorian' cast iron sectional column radiators
Ideal Clima 'Classic' & 'Tema' cast iron radiators
Bisque Arbonia
Etal Eurotherm aluminium sectional radiators
Vogue 'traditional' towel rails & bathroom heaters
Retting underfloor heating

Technical Literature:

Full range of technical literature available free of charge

Technical Advice:

Free design service to domestic & commercial clients, offering
assistance with sizes, output & style of radiators

UAHS ref no. S 51

Supplier – CAST IRON RADIATORS

G W Monson & Sons Ltd.
18 Ballyblack Road
Newtownards
Co. Down BT22 2AP

Telephone: 01247 812350   **Fax:** 01247 818559

Contact: Alan Murphy

Goods / materials supplied throughout Northern Ireland

Product Details: Cast iron 'school type' central heating radiators
Steel column radiators and towel rails
Boilers, pumps & general heating & plumbing equipment

Technical Literature: Free technical & design literature for radiators & heating
equipment

Technical Advice: Assistance with correct sizing & selection of heating equipment

UAHS ref no. S 56

Supplier – Architectural Salvage

Barewood Limited
176 Laws Court
North Street
Belfast BT1 1AS

Telephone: 01232 245618   **Fax:** 01232 245618

Contact: Veronica Kane

Goods / materials supplied throughout Ireland, UK and Europe

Product Details: Reclaimed antique pine doors, floors, architrave, skirting and furniture
Reclaimed bricks, slates and sandstone
Paint stripping service

UAHS ref no. S 29

Supplier – ARCHITECTURAL SALVAGE

Hastings White
94 Duneoin Road
Glarryford
Ballymena
Co. Antrim BT44 9HH

Telephone: 01266 685444   **Fax:** 01266 685444
Mobile: 0860 675908

Contact: Mr Hastings White

Goods/Materials supplied throughout Northern Ireland

Product Details: Reclaimed Bangor blue slates & ridge tiles
Rosemary & other clay roof tiles
Reclaimed bricks in all colours
Reclaimed timber beams inc. oak & pitch pine
Reclaimed hardwood & softwood flooring – beech, oak, maple, walnut, mahogany
Reclaimed flags, quarry tiles, cobble stones and sundry other goods
Antique chimney pots
Granite kerbs

UAHS ref no. S 61

Supplier – ARCHITECTURAL SALVAGE

O'Kane Reclamation
5 Mussenden Road
Castlerock
BT51 4RP

Telephone: 01265 849024 or   **Fax:** 01265 849024
01265 849225

Contact: Daniel O'Kane

Goods / material supplied throughout Ireland

Product Details: Bangor blue slates, quarry tiles, clay bricks & chimney pots, reclaimed flooring & doors, general architectural salvage, pine & oak beams

Technical Advice: Free advice on choice of suitable materials, building procedures & techniques

UAHS ref no. S 12

Supplier – ARCHITECTURAL SALVAGE

Peninsula Architectural Salvage
37 Ballyblack Road
Newtownards
Co. Down BT22 2AR

Telephone: 01247 822722
Mobile: 0498 525024

Goods/Materials supplied throughout Northern Ireland

Product Details: Reclaimed Bangor blue slates and ridge tiles
Rosemary and all other clay roof tiles
All types of reclaimed brick, quarry tiles, cobble stones, flag stones and kerb stones
All types of floors and doors made to order from reclaimed timber

UAHS ref no. S 63

Supplier – ARCHITECTURAL SALVAGE

Wilson's Conservation Building Products Ireland
123 Hillsborough Road
Dromore
Co. Down BT25 1QW

Telephone: 01846 692304   **Fax:** 01846 698322

Contact: Geoff or Rosie Wilson

Goods / materials supplied throughout Ireland & Europe

Product Details: Reclaimed Bangor blue slates & ridge tiles
Rosemary & other clay roof tiles
Reclaimed bricks inc. handmade bricks, & clay facing &
decorative bricks
Reclaimed timber beams inc. oak & pitch pine
Reclaimed hardwood & softwood flooring in strip & woodblock
inc. oak & maple
Reclaimed flags, quarry tiles, cobble stones & sundry other goods

Technical Advice: Free advice on laying, fitting & building procedures

UAHS ref no. S 9

APPENDIX 1: FURTHER READING

The following **Historic Buildings Technical Notes** are available free of charge from Environment and Heritage Service: Built Heritage, 5–33 Hill Street, Belfast BT1 2LA, tel. 01232 235000, fax. 01232 543111.

2	Thatch
3	Eaves details
4	Cobbles
5	Mortars – the manufacture of lime putty
14	Conservation of historic glass
15	Stained glass in N, Ireland
32	Signs and sign writing on historic buildings
35	Fanlights
36	Photographing historic buildings
37	Re-pointing of stonework
38	Cleaning stonework
39	Stonework repairs
41	Bolection moulding
42	Chimneys, flues and hearths
43	Roofs
44	Roof drainage
45	Masonry walls
46	Wall finishes – external
47	Wall finishes – internal
48	Windows and doors
49	Ferrous metal
50	Paint
51	Fire protection and thermal insulation
52	Cleaning masonry buildings (brick, stone and external renders)
53	Flood lighting of buildings
54	Glazed external protection for buildings
55	Value Added Tax and Listed buildings
57	Information on historic buildings grant
58	Guidance when planning cabled services

The following modestly priced publications are highly recommended by the Society; enquiries regarding cost should be directed to the relevant organisation. Each pamphlet contains a short bibliography relating to the topic discussed which will provide the reader with further valuable information.

The Society for the Protection of Ancient Buildings
37 Spital Square
London E1 6DY
Telephone: 0171 377 1644   Fax: 0171 247 5296

Technical Pamphlets

14/1   Outward leaning walls

14/2   Strengthening timber floors

14/5   Pointing stone and brick walling

14/8   The control of damp in old buildings

14/9   Electrical installation (Revised)

14/10 The care and repair of thatched roofs

14/11 Panel infilling to timber framed buildings

14/12 The repair of timber frames and roofs

14/14 Timber bell-frames

Information Sheets

IN/1   Basic limewash

IN/2   Timber treatment – a warning about the de-frassing of timbers

IN/3   The surface treatment of timber framed houses

IN/4   The need for old buildings to 'breathe'

IN/5   Removing paint from old buildings

IN/7   First aid repair to traditional farm buildings

IN/8   Tuck pointing in practice

IN/9   An introduction to building limes

IN/10 Patching old floorboards

IN/11 Rough-cast for historic buildings

IN/12 Introduction to the repair of lime-ash and plaster floors

The Georgian Group
6 Fitzroy Square
London W1P 6DX
Telephone: 0171 387 1720 Fax: 0171 387 1721

Guides

1 Windows
   The history and replacement of windows in Georgian buildings
2 Brickwork
   The types and repair of Georgian brickwork
3 Doors
   The history and care of Georgian doors and porches
4 Paint colour
   The colour and application of paint in Georgian houses
5 Render, stucco and plaster
   The history and maintenance of Georgian renders and plasters
6 Wallpaper
   The history, design and restoration of Georgian wallpaper
7 Mouldings
   Georgian mouldings
8 Ironwork
   Georgian ironwork
9 Fireplaces
   Georgian fireplaces
10 Roofs
   Georgian roofs and their treatment
11 Floors
   Georgian floors, their coverings and their treatment
12 Stonework
   The development and repair of Georgian stonework
13 Lighting
   The lighting of Georgian houses
14 Curtains and blinds
   The development and reconstruction of Georgian window treatments
15 Papier maché
   The history and maintenance of Georgian papier maché

The Victorian Society
1 Priory Gardens, London W4 1TT
Telephone: 0181 994 1019   Fax: 0181 995 4895

Care for Victorian and Edwardian Houses
A series of eight page illustrated A4 booklets which explain how to care for Victorian and Edwardian houses.

1   Doors
     Internal and external doors, fireproofing, door furniture, finishes etc.
2   Decorative tiles
     Care, repair and replacement of floor, wall and fireplace tiles
3   Fireplaces
     How to restore flues, fireplaces and surrounds
4   Interior mouldings
     Timber architraves, dado and picture rails, plaster cornices and roses
5   Wallcoverings
     Dadoes, fillings and friezes explained
6   Cast iron
     Decorative ironwork in Victorian and Edwardian houses
7   Brickwork
     Polychromy, pointing and damp-proofing
8   Paintwork
     History and choice of internal and external colour schemes for Victorian and Edwardian houses

Historic Scotland
Scottish Conservation Bureau
Longmore House, Salisbury Palace
Edinburgh EH9 1SH
Telephone: 0131 668 8668   Fax: 0131 668 8669
website: www.historic-scotland.gov.uk   email: cbrown.hs.scb@gtnet.gov.uk

Technical Advice Notes
TAN 1   Preparation & use of Lime Mortars
TAN 2   Conservation of plasterwork
TAN 3   Performance standards for timber sash and case windows
TAN 4   Thatch & thatching techniques
TAN 5   The Hebridean Blackhouse
TAN 6   Earth structures and construction in Scotland
TAN 7   Access to the Built heritage
TAN 8   Guide to International Conservation Charters
TAN 9   Stone cleaning of granite buildings
TAN 10   Biological growth on sandstone buildings; control and treatment
TAN 11   Fire protection measures in Scottish historic buildings
TAN 12   Quarries of Scotland
TAN 13   Archaeology of Scottish thatch

English Heritage
Customer Services Department
PO Box 9019
London W1A 0JA
Telephone: 0171 973 3434

English Heritage produce a large number of publications, all of which are described in their free Publication Catalogue.

The following are of particular relevance:

Practical building conservation

1   Stone masonry
2   Brick, terracotta & earth
3   Mortars, plasters and renders
4   Metals
5   Wood, glass and resins

Free Conservation Leaflets

English Heritage produce free leaflets on aspects of practical conservation, written for architects, planners, archaeologists and other professionals in the conservation field, as well as for a wider audience.

Conservation Bulletin is published three times a year and is available free to those actively involved in conservation. (The information refers specifically to England and not to Northern Ireland)

APPENDIX 2: GRANTS AND OTHER ASSISTANCE

Historic Buildings Grant
In some cases owners of listed buildings can obtain grant aid from the Environment and Heritage Service. Grants may be given towards the cost of the repair and maintenance of historic elements and associated professional fees. The Historic Buildings grants scheme changes from time to time and for current information and advice on grant assistance you should enquire at the Environment and Heritage Service office at 5–33 Hill Street, Belfast, BT1 2LA, (Tel. 01232 235000, Fax. 01232 543111). In order not to jeopardise an application, work on a project should not commence until an offer of grant assistance has been made.

Environment and Heritage Service may also be able to provide historical information and technical advice to owners. This can include advice on the acceptability of proposed works and information on historically correct materials and detailing. This is an advisory service, and it is recommended that, where an owner proposes to carry out works, consultants experienced in this specialist area are employed.

Conservation Area Grant
If you own a building in a Conservation Area, the Department of the Environment may grant aid expenditure relating to works either to listed or non-listed buildings that promote the preservation or enhancement of the character or appearance of the Conservation Area. External elements including chimneys, gutters and windows are eligible for grant aid. Further details may be obtained from your local Divisional Planning Office.

Renovation Grant
The Northern Ireland Housing Executive may grant aid the cost of improvement and conversion subject to means testing. In certain circumstances the Executive may also grant aid repair. Such grants do not necessarily exclude either Historic Buildings grant or Conservation Area grant, which should also be applied for as appropriate. Further details may be obtained from your local Northern Ireland Housing Executive office. The telephone numbers are listed on page 231 of the current Telephone Directory.

Urban Development Programme
Sponsored by the International Fund for Ireland (IFI), the purpose of this programme is to generate viable economic activity in derelict or vacant buildings or sites in the commercial centres of towns and villages in Northern Ireland, particularly where new jobs may be created. It may also be available for certain projects which improve the physical fabric of run-down areas and improve the economic infrastructure for the benefit of the wider community. Further details may be obtained from The Urban Development Programme (see Appendix 3 for address).

Northern Ireland Tourist Board
The Northern Ireland Tourist Board has a rural cottages initiative which has, in the past, restored buildings of character for conversion to self-catering holiday accommodation. Information on Leader and NITB grant assistance and general advice on rural cottage development is available from Anne McLoughlin, Rural Cottage Holidays, St Anne's Court, Belfast, BT1 1NB, Tel. 01232 895529, Fax. 01232 241198.

Hearth Revolving Fund
This charitable trust operates a revolving fund for the acquisition and restoration of historic buildings at risk, and is particularly interested in buildings in Conservation Areas. Further details may be obtained from Hearth Revolving Fund, 66 Donegall Pass, Belfast, BT7 1BU, Tel. 01232 530121, Fax. 01232 530122.

Charitable Trusts
Charitable trusts are sometimes willing to help with the conservation of buildings in charitable or other non profit-making ownership. Reference could usefully be made to the publication, A guide to the major trusts marketed by English Heritage and available in most large libraries (ISBN 0 907164 61 7).

Ulster Architectural Heritage Society
The Ulster Architectural Heritage Society, with some 1,200 members, is a voluntary body concerned with the promotion of good architecture of all periods in the nine counties of Ulster. As well as publishing many books and monographs concerning aspects of local architecture, it organises visits and lectures for its members, and is able to give technical advice of a general nature and can direct enquirers to appropriate sources of information. Further details can be obtained from the Secretary, UAHS, 66 Donegall Pass, Belfast, BT7 1BU, Tel. 01232 550213, Fax. 01232 550214.

APPENDIX 3: USEFUL ADDRESSES AND TELEPHONE NUMBERS

Listed Buildings and Historic Buildings Grants
Information, advice and grant application forms:

Environment and Heritage Service
5–33 Hill Street
Belfast BT1 2LA
Tel: 01232 235000

The Monuments and Buildings Record, which contains written information, photographs and drawings relating to historic buildings, structures and archaeological monuments and sites, is at the same address and telephone number. It is open to the public during office hours, Monday – Friday, 9.30 – 4.00.

CRISP schemes, Conservation Area Grant & Planning Issues
Contact should be made with the relevant Divisional Planning Office:

Ballymena Divisional Planning Office, Tel: 01266 653333, Fax: 01266 662127
Belfast Divisional Planning Office, Tel: 01232 252800, Fax: 01232 252828
Craigavon Divisional Planning Office, Tel: 01762 341144, Fax: 01762 341065
Coleraine Divisional Planning Office, Tel: 01265 41300, Fax: 01265 41434
Downpatrick Divisional Planning Office, Tel: 01396 612211, Fax: 01396 618196
Enniskillen Sub-Divisional Planning Office, Tel: 01365 327270, Fax: 01365 328016
Londonderry Divisional Planning Office, Tel: 01504 319900, Fax: 01504 319777
Newry Regeneration Project, Tel: 01693 250303
Omagh Divisional Planning Office, Tel: 01662 254000, Fax: 01662 254010

Urban Development Programme
Room 505
Londonderry House
21 / 27 Chichester Street
Belfast BT1 4JB
Tel: 01232 252500, Fax: 01232 252721

Northern Ireland Housing Executive
Advice and financial assistance
The address and telephone number of your local Home Improvement Grants Office can be obtained from:

The Housing Centre
2 Adelaide Street
Belfast BT2 8PB
Tel: 01232 240588 or on page 231 of the current Telephone Directory

The Architectural Heritage Fund
Low cost loans and feasibility study funding for existing charitable bodies:

The Secretary
The Architectural Heritage Fund
Clareville House
26 / 27 Oxendon Street
London SW1Y 4EL
Tel: 0171 925 0199, Fax: 0171 930 0295, E-mail: ahf@ahfund.co.uk; www.ahfund.co.uk

A copy of Funds for Historic Buildings in England and Wales is available from The Architectural Heritage Fund at a cost of £15.00. A similar directory is currently being prepared for Northern Ireland by The Environment and Heritage Society and should be available from late 1998.

The Heritage Lottery Fund
Guidelines, advice and application forms:

Heritage Lottery Fund
7 Holbein Place
London SW1W 8NR
Tel: 0171 591 6000
Fax: 0171 591 6001

Building Preservation Trusts
Advice and information regarding the setting up of a charitable trust:

The UK Association of Building Preservation Trusts (A.P.T.)
Clareville House
26 / 27 Oxendon Street
London SW1Y 4EL
Tel: 0171 930 1629, Fax: 0171 930 0295

Shane McBreen
A.P.T. (N.I.) Area Committee
6 Moygannon Court
Warrenpoint
Newry
Co. Down BT34 3JW
Tel: 016937 52700

The following four Building Preservation Trusts are interested in acquiring or leasing historic buildings in need of rescue:

Hearth Revolving Fund
66 Donegall Pass
Belfast BT7 1BU
Tel: 01232 530121

Ulster Churches Trust
c/o Cleaver Fulton & Rankin
Solicitors
50 Bedford Street
Belfast BT2 7FW
Tel: 01232 243141

Belfast Buildings Preservation Trust
c/o Belfast Civic Trust
Bryson House
28 Bedford Street
Belfast BT2 7FE
Tel: 01232 238437

Lecale Building Preservation Trust
c/o 38 Castle Street
Killough
Co. Down BT30 7QQ

Foyle Civic Trust
16B The Diamond
Londonderry BT48 6HW
Tel: 01504 372665

Inner City Trust
10–16 Pump Street
Derry BT48 6JG
Tel: 01504 260329

Northern Ireland Voluntary Trust
Advice about the European Programme for Peace & Reconciliation

Northern Ireland Voluntary Trust
22 Mount Charles
Belfast BT7 1NZ
Tel: 01232 245972
Fax: 01232 329839

The Rural Development Council for Northern Ireland
Advice and assistance for community and voluntary groups involved with rural regeneration projects:

The Rural Development Council
Loy Street
Cookstown
Co. Tyrone BT80 8PE
Tel: 016487 66980
Fax: 016487 66922

Rural Community Network
45 James Street
Cookstown
Co. Tyrone BT80 8AA
Tel: 016487 66670
Fax: 016487 66006

Department of Agriculture for Northern Ireland
Advice and assistance for farmers and rural land-owners:

Countryside Management Division
Department of Agriculture
Dundonald House
Upper Newtownards Road
Belfast BT4 3SB
Tel: 01232 524713 / 520100

The Irish Landmark Trust
The Trust is interested in restoring and converting unusual historic properties for holiday
accommodation:

The Irish Landmark Trust
23 St. Stephen's Green North
Dublin 2
Tel: 00 353 1 6766093
Fax: 00 353 1 6766094

Rural Cottage Holidays Ltd.
An organisation which leases and restores vernacular rural buildings for holiday
accommodation in partnership with the owner:

Rural Cottage Holidays Ltd.
St. Anne's Court
59 North Street
Belfast BT1 1NB
Tel: 01232 231221
Fax: 01232 240960

INDEX OF CRAFTSMEN, FIRMS, PRACTICES AND SUPPLIERS

INDEX OF CRAFTSMEN, FIRMS, PRACTICES AND SUPPLIERS contd.

INDEX OF SKILLS AND SPECIALISMS

INDEX OF SKILLS AND SPECIALISMS contd.

Above: Cliff consolidation for The National Trust at Downhill

Back Cover: Photograph courtesy of The Northern Builder